THE
DE BONO
CODE™ BOOK

Edward de Bono

VIKING

VIKING

Published by the Penguin Group
Penguin Books Ltd, 27 Wrights Lane, London W8 5TZ, England
Penguin Putnam Inc., 375 Hudson Street, New York, New York 10014, USA
Penguin Books Australia Ltd, Ringwood, Victoria, Australia
Penguin Books Canada Ltd, 10 Alcorn Avenue, Toronto, Ontario, Canada M4V 3B2
Penguin Books India (P) Ltd, 11, Community Cente,
Panchsheel Park, New Delhi – 110 017, India
Penguin Books (NZ) Ltd, Private Bag 102902, NSMC, Auckland, New Zealand
Penguin Books (South Africa) (Pty) Ltd, 5 Watkins Street,
Denver Ext 4, Johannesburg 2094, South Africa

Penguin Books Ltd, Registered Offices: Harmondsworth, Middlesex, England

First published 2000
1 3 5 7 9 10 8 6 4 2

Set in 10/14pt Monotype Optima
Typeset by Rowland Phototypesetting Ltd,
Bury St Edmunds, Suffolk
Printed in Great Britain by Clays Ltd, St Ives plc

A CIP catalogue record for this book is available from the British Library

Hardback ISBN 0-670-88848-6
Trade paperback ISBN 0-670-88849-4

Something of the sort is going to happen sooner or later. That is a mathematical certainty.

The 'sooner' will depend on those people who are able to understand what it is all about and to see the need and value.

The 'later' will be influenced by those who are unable to understand the concept and are outraged by it. They will seek to impose this sad ignorance on everyone else.

Language has been the biggest help in human progress.

Language is now by far the biggest barrier to human progress.

If language has indeed been the biggest help to human progress how can it now be the biggest barrier?

Language has enabled the human species to move ahead of primates even though there is only a tiny difference in genetic DNA. Language has allowed communication and therefore cooperation. Language has allowed the storing of knowledge so that future generations can benefit from the learning and wisdom of past generations. Language allows the formulation and expression of thoughts. Language allows competent and subtle descriptions.

So how can language now be the biggest barrier to human progress?

Any self-organizing system like human thought and human language reaches a stable equilibrium state (sometimes called a local equilibrium). It is very difficult to budge from this state because any change seems inferior. So we are sucked back to the equilibrium state. That is why changes in language are so slow and so difficult.

Purely on this system basis it is inevitable that language will reach a complacent 'stable' state and will become more and more inadequate at describing an increasingly complex world.

So language may indeed have been the biggest help towards human progress up to this point in time. It may also be the biggest barrier to further progress. A child's clothes are important and suitable but the child eventually grows out of them. The clothes remain wonderful but their value is changed. Trainer wheels on a bicycle are essential until you learn to ride the bicycle – but a hindrance thereafter.

The apparent contradiction can also be resolved in another way. Language as a general concept remains as valuable as it has always been. At the

4

same time, our current language is a barrier to progress. That is why this book needed to be written.

Language is an encyclopedia of ignorance. Words and concepts enter language at a state of relative ignorance (relative to our current knowledge). These perceptions are frozen into permanence with a language word. So we are forced to perceive the world in a very old-fashioned way. It is for precisely this reason that language has become a barrier to human progress. For example, the perception of 'profit' has severely limited the social development of business and value creation in society.

Why, then, have we not been able to develop the new concepts and perceptions that are needed? The answer to this question is the key element in the whole book.

We have not developed new perceptions or complex perceptions because our ability to describe in words is so superb that we feel we can describe any situation perfectly well with the existing language.

This is a dangerous and fatal mistake because description and perception are two different things.

Description is not perception

As I have mentioned in a previous book of mine, some Inuit languages in Canada have one word which says, 'I like you very much but I would not go seal hunting with you.'

You can look across a table and 'see' someone through that perception. This is totally different from saying after the meeting: 'Joe is a good fellow and I like him, but I would not want to go seal hunting with him.' Description after the event is not at all the same as perception at the time.

As a matter of fact I think this powerful Inuit word is not good enough. Two words are needed:
1. 'I like you very much but I would not want to go seal hunting with you because you do not pull your weight (make holes in the ice, lug the seals, etc., etc.)
2. 'I like you very much but I would not want to go seal hunting with you because we should be spending hours together on the ice and you are very boring company!'

Imagine the following shape: there are three lines; at each of its ends one line joins another line to form an angle; the three angles so formed enable the three lines to enclose an area completely.

Would it not be very much simpler if we had the word 'triangle'? Description is not perception.

Imagine a huge chest with lots of drawers. Each drawer contains one type of word. Whenever we want to describe anything we open the appropriate drawers and take out the required words. When we have finished we return the words to the drawers. What has been described has an existence only while we assemble the words to describe it.

Description follows perception. But what guides that perception?

Australia, Thailand, USA, Argentina, Singapore, Hong Kong, Kuwait, Copenhagen, London was the itinerary of a recent trip of mine. The itinerary exists only when the travel agent has put it together.

Contrast that with the concept of 'Amsterdam'. That immediately conjures up canals, practical, easy-going people, window-shopping for sex, brown cafés, etc.

A concept has its ramifications and its suburbs – just like a town.

A concept or a word has its own 'locus' (or place) in the nerve networks of the mind; from this locus we move more easily to other places. A description is an itinerary which visits one place after another. In neurological terms the two are totally different.

The brain can see only what it is prepared to see. If the brain contains complex concepts then we can perceive the world through these concepts: this is perception.

The Xhosa language in Africa has twenty-six different words for the horns of an animal. This makes recognition and identification of animals much easier and more definite. All this is very different from description after the event.

So how are we going to create the new words that are going to allow us to see the world in a much richer and much more powerful way?

Grotesque and bizarre

Creating new words will always seem bizarre and grotesque. I created the term 'lateral thinking', which is now well accepted and is to be found in dictionaries, television sitcoms and movies (*Metro*, for example).

But the word 'po', which is much more important, has been slow to catch on. 'Po' signals 'this is a provocation; see where your mind moves on to from this provocation.' 'Po' is more important because any self-organizing system, like the brain, forms asymmetric patterns and there is an absolute need for provocation in order to cut across patterns. Provocation is an essential operation in creativity.

We eventually form new words for new things like computers and the Internet because these are visible and around us. It is very much harder to form new words first so that we can then see things in a new way.

So how can we enrich the perception ability of the human brain if it is so difficult to form new words?

To create the new concepts and perceptions we use numbers. This is not much different from using a telephone number to gain access to a person.

There is also the powerful benefit that numbers are international.

SHOCK, HORROR AND OUTRAGE

Sadly, I fully expect the concepts put forward in this book to be treated with shock, horror and hysterical outrage by those word merchants who believe that language is perfect and complete.

Word games in the manner of traditional philosophy are no longer enough. To understand the human brain it is necessary to understand neural networks, self-organizing systems and biological systems.

Ask any mathematician whether a brain consisting of just five neurones would be capable of fifty thousand million thoughts, and the mathematician would laugh in your face. And yet, using a simple biological factor (not available to engineers), it is very simple. The factor is the 'tiring factor' – the key factor in brain organization.

Those who do not understand these things are both furious and floundering. They end up not reviewing the content of the book at all but reviewing their own peevish attitude to me. This is an insult to their readers who would prefer to learn about the book. It is a disgrace that literary editors permit such rubbish. In an effort to be clever such reviews end up by being pathetically absurd in the eyes of those who know my work and have read the book in question.

There have been sensitive and thoughtful reviews of my books by people like Anthony Burgess but (in the UK) reviews are mostly feeble rubbish.

Such limited intelligences will not see the biological need for a higher-order language. They will seek to sneer at 'making love by numbers' or some other such cleverism.

It was Einstein who said that any really new idea had to provoke outrage from those who could not understand it. So, in a way, the absurdity of the anticipated outrage will be flattering.

After a long journey abroad I returned early one morning to Heathrow airport. In the British Airways arrival lounge I checked in to have a shower. As I gave my name an attendant standing nearby asked if I was the 'de Bono' who wrote the books. I said I was.

'I read all of them,' he said. 'So refreshing.' That compliment from an apparently ordinary person means more to me than endless rubbish from mediocre intellectuals.

BENEFITS

Benefit 1: International

As communication and business become ever more global the language differences become ever more important. Most people may learn enough English (as the commonest language) to get by conversationally. But describing complex concepts is another matter.

When matters get complex there is a need for a skilled interpreter and a rush to the dictionary. All this is simplified by the de Bono code (only some of which is given in this book).

The code forms an 'inter-language'. You think into the code in English, the other person thinks out of the code in Chinese. Indeed you could think into the code in English and one person might think out of the code in Chinese, another person in German, another person in Korean, another person in Urdu – all at the same time. Every person learns the codes in his or her own language. The numbers are international. All that is necessary is that the code books are available in the other languages.

For the first time in history it becomes possible to communicate complex concepts across language boundaries.

The same applies to the travel code – a version of which is given in this book. The traveller thinks into a 'code number' and the listener thinks out of the number into his or her own language.

Benefit 2: Perception

As I have emphasized already, perception is not description. The brain can only see what it is prepared to see. With the codes a complex perception has its own 'locus' in the brain.

With the codes it becomes possible to 'see' complex situations at a glance. It becomes possible to communicate them and to deal with them. This raises human interaction to a much higher level than has ever been possible before. Those who cannot see the difference between description and perception will be unable to see the immense value of this point.

Benefit 3: Complex Concepts

There is no limit to the complexity that may be put into a single code. The code comes to cover all the complexity in one 'bite'.

In the mood code 10/15 means: 'I am upset and not pleased in a general sense. I am not happy with the way things are going. There is no one person or event about which I am unhappy. It is a general response to what I see happening.'

Complex concepts can indicate a very special set of circumstances. There could even be a code for 'irritating your neighbour's dog in the house on the right.' There is not, but there could be.

Benefit 4: New Concepts

Only some of the codes are given in this introductory book. There are other codes which would be specially applicable in the business world.

The code system allows the introduction of a new code at any time. This is very much faster than language, where the introduction of new concepts is extremely slow and difficult.

We could have a concept for politicians as follows: 'You are making necessary public noises. You are expected to make these noises. We know you do not believe in them. We know that you know that we know that you do not believe in them. But the noises are expected.'

We could have a code for book reviewers as follows: 'You do not begin to understand this book so your only option is to be bitchy in the hope that it will seem clever and hide your stupidity.'

Benefit 5: Precision

Because the complex concepts can be exact and detailed it becomes possible to be very precise. For example, in the relationship code 14/2 is very different from 14/5.

This precision means that differences of perception can be pinpointed. If one party sees the situation as 14/2 but the other sees it as 14/5, then the difference can be discussed.

When concepts are broad and vague they include so much that quite different situations may come under broad concepts such as 'negotiation'. The negotiation code breaks down this broad concept into much more precise concepts.

If all birds came under the general concept of 'birds' then we would have a problem distinguishing a canary from a lorikeet. Because birds have different names (and different species names) we can be much more precise. At the moment we are very much better at naming birds and plants than at naming human situations.

Benefit 6: Expectations

This is something which ordinary language does not do at all. You have to wait until something has been said or read in order to know what it is all about.

The 'pre-code' indicates in advance the general nature of what is coming. This allows the 'mindset' to prepare itself.

The 'information code' classifies information so that we know at once what sort of information is presented. The 'reply code' indicates the reply very succinctly.

The codes signal in advance 'what this is all about'.

Benefit 7: Avoiding Awkwardness

There are times when feelings are clear enough but it is awkward or embarrassing to express them directly. The codes can provide a simple, neutral and direct way of signalling feelings.

The 'youth code' allows youngsters to communicate more directly with their parents – and the other way around. Youngsters often find it difficult to express themselves. The code simplifies this.

The 'mood code' makes it possible to signal a mood directly rather than hope that those around you can detect your mood from your behaviour. It also makes it acceptable to show your feelings.

The 'relationship codes' provide a means for the parties involved to express their feelings and thoughts about the relationship in a direct way without risk of causing offence.

In general, the neutrality of the codes reduces aggression, shyness and awkwardness. Matters which might not have been discussed before can now be discussed.

The 'meetings code' is a very clear example of a type of communication that would simply not be possible without the code. Without the code such communication would be rude, impertinent and disruptive. The code makes it simple, acceptable and very useful.

Benefit 8: Saving Time

In many cases what is expressed in a code could have been discussed in normal language – but it would have taken very much longer. So the codes save time.

For example, the 'attention-directing codes' are short and simple, and guide thinking. To do this without some form of coding would be cumbersome and tedious.

With the rapidly growing use of the Internet there is a danger of information overload. The codes are a way of saving time. To be able to indicate something with a short code is a big advantage over having to describe it in full each time.

Benefit 9: Information Management

Just as there is a saving of time with the codes, so also is there a saving of space.

The codes are of value in general information management because they are short, direct and succinct. One could imagine a very comprehensive interchange taking place almost entirely in code on both sides. The subject would need to be specified in ordinary language but thereafter the situations and processes could all be carried by the codes.

17

Every word in language is a code which triggers a pattern in the brain. The codes are more complex words which trigger more complex patterns. The benefits for information management are obvious.

Benefit 10: Uniformity

Whenever people use ordinary language to describe a complex situation there is a danger that different words might be used, different nuances and even different intonations. So the same situation is no longer the same situation when it is described by different people. There may be far too much subjective input.

The codes are neutral and finite. There is no room for subjective input. You may be subjective about which code you wish to use but once chosen the code is fixed and unchangeable.

As suggested above, the great value of classification in botany (and geology, etc.) is its uniformity. When a name is used that name always means exactly the same type of plant. If there are significant variations then a new name is given to the 'different' plant.

Benefit 11: Calm

Usually, feelings, emotions and behaviour are very much part of our communication repertoire. People around us are expected to pick up clues from facial expressions, tone of voice, etc. Unless the emotional component is there the message may not get across. Dogs growl. Monkeys bare their teeth. Surely human beings can evolve a little further?

The codes allow matters to be expressed in complete calm. The judge in a court delivers the sentence in complete calm. The judge does not exhibit the rage society may be feeling towards the criminal. But the calmly delivered sentence is real enough. The instruction to release a nuclear bomb may be very calmly given.

With the current reliance on visible emotional communication, those who are not good at this are at a disadvantage. They cannot pump themselves up into anger. With the codes everyone is on a level playing field.

Benefit 12: Locus

Research on people with strokes or head injury has shown that everything is very precisely located in the brain. After a stroke, for example, one man lost only the ability to remember the names of vegetables – nothing else.

In time, the most-used codes will come to have their own place or 'locus' in the brain. We shall then be able to see the world in a very much richer way.

When you look at a painting and recognize that it is by Edvard Munch, it is because the colour, composition, style, expression, etc., have all been coded under the name Edvard Munch. In the same way, we shall now be able to recognize and communicate complex situations. Human evolution will be able to move beyond the existing language barrier.

This book contains two codes:

de Bono code A

de Bono code B.

For entirely logical reasons, which will become apparent later, code B will come first and code A will follow.

PRONUNCIATION USAGE

Where it is possible or convenient to use the term 'de Bono code' this is the most sure way of indicating that the code is being used.

In writing it may be cumbersome to use the full description, so 'dBc' could be used.

Instead of any such indicator it is possible to indicate de Bono code B by simply putting a '0' before the code. So 14/5 would be 014/5. In time this might become clear enough.

Code A will be distinguished from code B by having '00' in front.

In speech the numbers before the slash of code B are always pronounced as full numbers. The numbers after the slash are also pronounced as full numbers. So 12/10 is pronounced as 'twelve ten'. Code 14/13 is pronounced as 'fourteen thirteen'.

With code A each digit is pronounced separately. So 783 is pronounced as 'seven eight three'.

There is an international code for numbers that will be described later. This will allow numbers, which are already international visually, to become international aurally too.

Part 1

DE BONO CODE B

OVERVIEW OF THE CODES FROM DE BONO CODE B THAT ARE INCLUDED IN THIS BOOK

Code 1: Pre-Code

This code indicates in advance what the following message or communication is about. Like putting the question mark at the beginning of the sentence in Spanish.

Code 2: Attention Directing

Thinking tools for deliberately directing attention in order to improve perception, where ninety per cent of the errors of thinking occur.

Code 3: Action Code

A quick code which is directed at action. Communication with others or oneself.

Code 4: Difficult Situations

The code classifies certain types of difficult situation so that these can be perceived and communicated. For example, a difficult environment in which to work.

Code 5: Response Code

A simplified and direct way of responding to inquiries, requests and questions. The code expresses the reply in a short manner.

Code 6: Interaction (Frantic) Code

A short code especially for dealing with 'frantic' situations between people. The code defuses the situation and removes the conflict element.

Code 7: Information Code

The code classifies types of information so we know what to expect and what to look for amongst the mass of information available.

Code 8: Youth Code

Youngsters sometimes find it difficult to express awkward and embarrassing situations. The code provides a means which is neutral and comprehensive. Can be used either way between adults and youngsters.

Code 9: Meetings

A code which allows participants at a meeting to signal their thoughts and feelings visually to the speaker so the speaker knows how they are reacting.

Code 10: Mood Code

People show their moods with facial expressions, tone of voice, behaviour and bad temper. The code provides a means of communicating a wide range of moods in a direct and quiet manner.

Code 11: Distance Code

This is a fun code which allows people to get to know each other at a distance through using the hand signals which carry code 11.

Code 12: Relationships Start

The code signals different messages, intentions and moods at the start of a relationship. Instead of fumblings for words, the code provides clarity between the parties.

Code 13: Relationships Continue

This code signals situations, moods and intentions in the course of an ongoing relationship. There are things which are difficult to express with words but easy with a situation code.

Code 14: Relationships End

The relationship is coming to an end. The relationship is breaking up. These are difficult times. The way things are expressed becomes very important. The code takes over that role.

Code 15: Negotiation

In the course of a negotiation there are things each party might want to say to the other. This code formalizes some of these requests so that they become part of the negotiating process. This removes tension and aggression.

Code 16: Assessment

This code deals with the assessment of people. It is a simple and impersonal way of commenting on performance: of praising good performance and noting bad performance.

Code 17: Project Status

How is the project doing? What is holding things up? The code formalizes and simplifies communication about the status of a project.

Code 18: Travel Code

The code deals with basic requests that might need to be made across a language barrier in the course of travel: seeking accommodation; needing medical help; advice on entertainment, etc.

PRE-CODE
CODE 1

Spanish may be the only language where a question mark is put at the beginning of a question. This is very sensible and very practical. You know in advance that a question is coming. Your 'mindset' is prepared for the question. In other languages you have to rely on the words used and the structure of the sentence.

There is a high value in having a 'pre-code' which indicates in broad terms what sort of communication you are about to receive.

Spoken language does not have any punctuation marks. We detect a question from the choice of words, the structure of the sentence and the rising tone of voice. A simple sentence becomes a question if the rising tone of voice indicates it: 'There was a positive response to your suggestion.'

Transferring from spoken language to written language leads to the question mark being put at the end of the sentence. But why should written language be just like spoken language?

With the growth of the Internet and e-mail there is a rapidly increasing use of written language for communication. A pre-code is of great value in written language.

Once the pre-code has been used in written communication it can feed back into oral communication.

A pre-code of some sort can simplify and add value to communication. We have waited long enough for one to evolve. It is now time to design one. This is code 1.

Code 1
Pre-Code

1/1 This is a friendly greeting. There is no request attached to it.

There are many general-purpose greetings. These are like sending a Christmas card. They are acknowledgements of the other person. They indicate a willingness to stay in touch.

Such communications are an offering of goodwill, of friendship. They are an indication that the person communicated with is part of the community of the communicator.

Such a communication may well include some information. For example: 'I went on holiday to the Seychelles' or 'My son graduated from college' or 'I have taken up goldfish breeding', etc.

Such information is not the main purpose of the communication but is incidental to it. The information just enlarges the greeting purpose of the communication.

It is very important to be clear that a 1/1 pre-code is intended as a greeting. That is how it will, and should, be taken.

With a 1/1 there is no obligation or expectation that the receiver will respond. The communicator is not laying this obligation on the receiver. It is like smiling at someone – but not expecting a smile back. A reply is not needed. Politeness does not demand a reply to a 1/1 communication.

CODE 1

1/2 This is a request for information on the matters indicated.

Questions are very often a request for information. A question really says, 'Direct your attention to this matter and give me information on it.' So when you ask, 'What is your name?' you are really saying, 'Direct your attention to your name and give me the relevant information.'

It is essential to specify in the message itself, right after the code, exactly the area in which you want the information. You do need to indicate what information you want.

The use of the code 1/2 does not mean that you cannot use ordinary language to frame your question as well. The pre-code simply indicates the nature of what is coming.

> 1/2 Please let me have information on the Cook Islands. What is the best time of year to go there? How do I get there? Is it expensive? What are the hotels like?

In certain cases it might be enough to use the code alone.

> 1/2 flight time from London to Johannesburg.
> 1/2 training in de Bono thinking methods in Singapore.

There may be a whole list of things about which you want information – so you just list them.

Always remember that when asking for information you are imposing a burden on the receiver. So it is polite to be as specific as possible.

CODE 1

1/3 I need very specific and very detailed information on the matter indicated.

It is easy enough to say, 'I want all information about everything.' You are unlikely to get it. If you ask for too much you are likely to get too little. So how do you indicate the detail or depth of the information that you want?

Code 1/2 is a request for information. If, however, you really need detailed information then you have the practical possibility of indicating this with code 1/3.

> 1/3 information on medication for malaria prevention.
> 1/3 flights to Paris from London after 7 p.m.

As with 1/2 you can spell out in words exactly what you want. You can communicate as you would have done if code 1 had not existed. Then you add the code number to let the receiver know what to expect. The use of the code numbers is not intended to interfere with the use of language. Those very familiar with the codes may find they simplify and shorten communications.

CODE 1

1/4 This is a request for your response and your reaction to what is indicated here.

This is a general but deliberate request for the reaction of the other person:

'What do you feel about this?'

'What do you think about this?'

'How do you react to this?'

'How do you respond to this?'

A reaction is specifically requested. The type of reaction is left open. It may be a thinking reaction or it may be an emotional reaction. It may be an instant 'top of the head' reaction or it may be a deeply considered reaction.

Information is neutral but a personal reaction is personal. The personal response may be from an individual in his or her own right or it may be from an individual representing a business or a group.

'1/4 we sell you our Internet division.'

'1/4 we join up for the summer vacation.'

'1/4 our getting married this year.'

'1/4 we raise the price on our luxury brand.'

Reactions may be based on information, logic and emotion. The person responding may respond in a detailed way and give reasons for the response. Or the person may give a simple response without reasons.

CODE 1

1/5 Please expand on this. Please give the reasons behind this. Please explain. Please provide the perspective and background. How did you reach this conclusion?

There is a need to know how some conclusion was arrived at. What was the thinking involved? There is a need to know reasons and background.

1/5 your decision to pull out of the consortium.
1/5 the delay in settling this invoice.
1/5 the choice of Sardinia for a holiday.
1/5 the choice of law as a career.
1/5 the remark you made about my being stingy.
1/5 the investment in China.
1/5 the need to use the de Bono code.

Code 1/5 might occasionally be used after code 1/4 if it seems that the reaction needs explaining. It is also possible to use both together as: 1/4, 1/5. This would indicate: 'Give me your reaction but also explain the reasons behind this reaction.'

The elaboration and explanation does not simply have to be a logical support for a position. It is more a matter of establishing the context in which the position has emerged.

'I do not trust him.'
'We have had bad experiences in China.'
'Consumer products are not our business.'

CODE 1

1/5

These are not fully logical reasons but they do explain why a position has been taken. It is much more a matter of 'explaining' a position rather than 'justifying' the position.

Adequate detail is specifically requested.

CODE 1

1/6 I simply do not understand the following matter. Could you please clarify it for me? Could you please explain it in terms I can understand? What is this about?

This is a direct request for clarification. The matter that needs to be clarified has to be stated very clearly.

Obviously clarification and explanation overlap considerably. 1/6 is not asking for the reasons behind something (which is what 1/5 does) but is a request that the matter be made intelligible.

    1/6 the new pension plan contributions.
    1/6 the role of the 'innovations office'.
    1/6 what you want me to do about the mortgage.
    1/6 why it is important to have a tattoo.
    1/6 how I can order the specific product I want.
    1/6 how I can do my banking over the net.

Wherever there is ignorance, confusion, doubt and uncertainty the 1/6 code has a place.

As before, the use of 1/6 does not shut out the use of normal language. The code can simply be an addition to the language – to emphasize the nature of the communication.

CODE 1

1/7 *I want to draw your attention to the following matter. I want to bring the following matter to your attention. I want to place the following matter before you.*

There is no specific request for a response or a reaction. The receiver of the communication can react as he or she wishes.

You may want to bring to someone's attention a change in procedures, a change in government regulations or a change in pricing. The purpose of the communication is directly to inform the other party.

1/7 I shall be abroad for the next three months.
1/7 I have taken up a new position with the Environment Agency.
1/7 I am now in a position to handle a request for concept design.
1/7 the item [specify] that I ordered five weeks ago has not been delivered.
1/7 the union will oppose any change in overtime payments.

You may wish to make announcements, statements, declarations, etc. Or you may wish to draw attention to something which may have been overlooked.

CODE 1

1/8 This is a request that you lay out your action plans for the matter specified. What are you going to do? Please be specific and do not just respond with generalities. What steps are you taking in this matter?

This is a direct request for proposed action plans. What is going to be done? What are you going to do?

The specific steps need to be laid out. There is a direct request for specifics. It is not enough to say, 'I shall solve this problem by using the most appropriate solution.'

 1/8 your dog terrorizing our children.
 1/8 the sharp fall in sales in the last quarter.
 1/8 your clear infringement of my copyright.
 1/8 my request for a divorce.
 1/8 our Internet sales are being undercut by this new start-up.
 1/8 raising venture capital for the new communication code.

There is a request for 'information' on what the action plan or intended action might be. There is no attempt to direct, guide or suggest what actions ought to be taken. There is only the implied suggestion that some action is needed.

If no action plan is in place then the request is: 'to think about it; to formulate an action plan; and then to communicate that action plan'.

CODE 1

1/9 *This is a request that you carry out the action specified here. You are politely asked to carry out the action. You are even ordered to carry out the action.*

The action request is much more in the nature of a polite request than an order. At the same time, it is much stronger than a mere suggestion.

In code 1/8 the other party was asked for his or her action intentions. In code 1/9 the other party is told to act in a certain defined way.

1/9 is not a request for information. It is a transmission of a require-ment.

Obviously the action required has to be specified. This may be specified in detail. Or, the ultimate objective may be specified and the other party left to figure out how to achieve that objective.

> 1/9 seek out and acquire Internet start-ups in the legal field.
> 1/9 investigate the background of this new leader of the party.
> 1/9 meet me in St Tropez on 20 August.
> 1/9 change the date of the meeting to Monday week.
> 1/9 find out who the creative people are in the organization.
> 1/9 set up a foundation to use these funds for educational purposes.
> 1/9 find me the best four-wheel drive vehicle on the market.
> 1/9 make sure all our people use the de Bono code.

In both written and spoken language directives usually sound harsh and dictatorial. Do this. Do that. Orders are often resented even when they are

CODE 1

1/9

fully legitimate and needed. Because code 1/9 is artificial, neutral and impersonal there is less resentment.

You can still use phrases like: 'Would you mind . . .' or 'It would be a help if . . .' if you wish.

CODE 1

1/10 I am putting forward a proposal or suggestion for your consideration. I believe there is merit in these suggestions.

This is the opposite of an 'order'. There is no compulsion involved. There may be action suggestions, product proposals, solution alternatives, etc.

The person putting forward the proposals may have every right to do so (for example a product development team). The person may be an outsider who is pitching the proposals to someone.

The proposals should stand on their own feet. The nature of the proposals, the mechanisms for implementing them and the benefits should be clearly spelled out.

Code 1/10 does not automatically include a request for a response. The code simply indicates that proposals are to follow. If you want a reaction then code 1/4 can be used.

In all cases, putting forward unsolicited proposals does not impose on the receiver any obligation to respond.

> 1/10 we could seek a partner in India.
> 1/10 we could outsource our fabric design needs.
> 1/10 we could offer a high reward for information leading to the arrest and conviction of those involved.
> 1/10 we could sell up and move to a quieter life in the country.
> 1/10 there seem to be three choices for this season's colour: magenta, pearl grey and lime green.
> 1/10 there are these three choices for the chief executive job . . .
> 1/10 we could try to make friends with the neighbours.
> 1/10 you could advertise in the *Hindi Times* for a wife.

CODE 1

1/10

Proposals can range from the very sensible to the wildly creative. In all thinking and in all progress, 'possibilities' are key. Code 1/10 indicates very specifically that proposals are to follow.

CODE 1

1/11 I want to register a complaint. I want to bring this to your attention because I think you would like to know about it. If possible, I would appreciate a reply.

Complaints can range from fully justified complaints, as in the breakdown of a brand new car, to trivial complaints from people who are pernickety and enjoy complaining.

Code 1/11 clearly indicates that what follows is a complaint. Most organizations welcome feedback because it allows them to improve the quality of their service. There may also be things they do not yet know about.

The pre-code allows a person to launch directly into the substance of the complaint without a lengthy preamble.

The code also allows more domestic complaints, which can now be put forward as neutral statements rather than as personal attacks.

> 1/11 someone always leaves the cap off the toothpaste.
> 1/11 I always seem to get asked to do the washing up.
> 1/11 the walls of the hotel room allow too much sound through.
> 1/11 your sales assistant in the hardware section did not seem to know his job.
> 1/11 although you attend every meeting you never seem to contribute.
> 1/11 the budget cuts make it impossible to delivery quality.
> 1/11 the training in creativity is very old-fashioned.
> 1/11 the supervisor is a bully.

CODE 1

1/11

A genuine complaint always implies that something can be put right. It is not much use complaining that you are too short or too tall. But there may be a point in complaining that you are too fat. There may also be a point in complaining that door heights are too low for tall people.

The emphasis of code 1/11 is on a gentle constructive complaint rather than a fierce attack.

CODE 1

1/12 This is *a direct response to your request (specified)*.

This is a general response code. The request does need to be specified in terms of date, subject matter, etc.

This response can include any type of reply. There can be information, personal reactions, suggestions for action, options, etc. Even though many of these have their own codes there is no need to separate everything out. The response to a specific request can include whatever it needs to include. It would be pedantic and tiresome to have to classify the different aspects of the response.

Note that there is a specific 'reply code', which will be covered later. This 'reply code' allows certain standard types of reply to be given quickly and succinctly. There is some overlap with other codes but for a general-purpose response, code 1/12 indicates that what follows seeks to meet the requests made. The two codes can be combined where necessary.

1/12 your request about training . . .
1/12 your request for information about the Cook Islands . . .
1/12 my reaction to the proposed merger . . .
1/12 the action plan is as follows . . .
1/12 your proposal is of interest for the following reasons . . .
1/12 these are the reasons behind my decision . . .

In all cases the date of the request and some way of specifying the request should be given. Code 1/12 simply indicates that what follows is a reply and not a new matter that is being communicated.

CODE 1

1/12

The reply should fit the request. If clarification has been sought this should be given. If information has been sought then this should be given.

Code 1/12 indicates a genuine and direct attempt to respond. If you wish to respond in any other way it would be best to use the 'reply code'.

1/13 I wish to register a disagreement. What follows is a point of view which is different from the one you put forward. There is a disagreement with what is specified.

This is an advance warning that a disagreement is to follow. It is essential that the matter in dispute is specified very precisely.

1/13 your suggestion of price increases.
1/13 the Maldives as a holiday destination.
1/13 your choice of the new office manager.
1/13 your prediction of stock-market behaviour over the coming year.
1/13 the prevailing attitude towards the Internet.
1/13 the decriminalization of marijuana.
1/13 purchasing the property at . . .
1/13 your choice of career.

The reasons for the disagreement are then spelled out thoroughly. This can usually take two forms. The first form is attacking the reasons behind the choice and showing that the choice may have negative consequences. The second form consists of offering another alternative and showing why this is better.

This code is by no means essential but is a polite and impersonal way of signalling a disagreement.

CODE 1

1/14 This is the information which you requested. Here are the answers to your questions.

The request needs to be specified. It may help to repeat the questions and give an answer to each one of them.

1/14 obviously overlaps with 1/12, which is a 'general' response to a request. There are times, however, when it is important simply to indicate that only information is being given; 1/14 refers specifically and only to information.

'You asked for information. Here it is.'
'This is the information you wanted.'
'The answers to your questions follow . . .'

How much information is given is up to you. You may give more than has been requested. If, on the other hand, the asker has made too broad a request (send me all information on net auction companies) then you can either give some information or ask the person to be more specific.

CODE 1

1/15 Here is some information. This communication contains information. It has not been asked for but is offered to you because it may be of interest to you. It is unsolicited information.

The pre-code indicates that what follows is neither a request nor a response to a request. It is simply information that is being offered.

The type of information being offered may be coded by the 'information code', which will be covered later. If the information code is used then there is no need to use the 1/15 code as well.

The sender may choose to specify why the information may be of use to you. If not, you may choose to ignore communications of this sort.

If 1/15 communications are likely to be ignored then people might prefer not to use this pre-code. When the pre-code habit is well established, however, communications with no pre-code will be even more likely to be ignored.

1/15 may also be used with 1/7, which is a signal to draw someone's attention to information. This indicates that some importance or relevance attaches to the information.

CODE 1

1/16 This is a schedule, plan, timetable, action sequence, itinerary, layout, etc. This is information you need and may have asked for.

The information given here is much more specific than general information and there is a direct connection of 'need'.

1/16 the conference schedule.
1/16 the itinerary of the visit.
1/16 the sequenced action plan.
1/16 the stages in the legal process.
1/16 the steps to the next election.
1/16 the project implementation schedule.
1/16 the layout of the new warehouse.

There is usually some sequence or time factor. One thing follows on from another.

The code may also indicate a plan, like the layout of a building, where there is no time sequence.

ATTENTION DIRECTING
CODE 2

Thinking is the most fundamental of all human skills. The quality of our future will depend directly on the quality of our thinking. Is it then not only astonishing but also absurd that thinking is not the core subject in all education and the central subject on any school curriculum? It is not. It is not there at all. There are some schools that teach thinking. Many of them teach critical thinking, which is excellent but totally inadequate. Judgement thinking is important but so is design thinking. We need to create as well as to judge.

David Perkins at Harvard has shown that ninety per cent of errors in thinking are errors of perception. This has also been my experience over the thirty years in which I have been involved in the teaching of thinking. Yet over the ages we have put all the emphasis on logic.

If your perception is faulty, then even excellent logic will give you the wrong answer. Excellent logic will not, itself, provide excellent perception.

If your eyesight is very sharp but you are looking in the wrong direction you will not see what you are looking for.

An explorer is sent to a newly discovered island. The explorer returns and reports on a smoking volcano and a bird that does not fly. The backers of the explorer are not satisfied: 'What else was there?'

'That is all that caught my attention,' replies the explorer.

So the explorer is sent back again with some 'attention-directing' tools. The explorer is asked to 'look north and note what you see'. Then, 'look south and note what you see'. Then look east and west in the same way. Also make notes on: flora, fauna, geology, water, etc., etc. This becomes a sort of checklist.

We need 'attention-directing tools' for human perception. Many years ago I designed a set of such tools. They are now in use (as the CoRT programme) in thousands of schools around the world. They are also being taught in business through the DATT programme (operated by APTT).

In the Karee platinum mine in South Africa there used to be 210 fights every month between the seven different tribes working there. After the basic attention-directing tools were taught (by Susan Mackie and Donalda Dawson) the fights dropped from 210 to just four.

Jennifer O'Sullivan, in Australia, had two job clubs and every one of her unemployed youngsters was deaf. Teaching these youngsters CoRT thinking gave an employment rate more than double the average for job clubs.

In a pilot project with unemployed youngsters in the UK, the use of these methods by the Holst Group improved unemployment four- to fivefold.

Attention-directing tools are very powerful. If you are looking in the right direction you see things. Once you have seen something you cannot 'unsee' it. Your thinking, choices, decisions are determined by what you have seen.

So code 2 is a very simple set of attention-directing tools. You can instruct yourself to use a particular tool. You can ask someone else to use a particular tool. You can suggest to a group that a particular tool be used.

In a computer you might pull down a menu and then click on an item on that menu. The thinking tools are items on a 'thinking menu'.

Code 2
Attention Directing

(The Thinking Code)

2/1 Direct your attention to the 'plus' points, then to the 'minus' points and then to the 'interesting' points. Tell me what you see.

This code is the same as the PMI tool in both the CoRT programme and the DATT course.

We are inclined to make rapid judgements: 'I like this' and 'I don't like this.' We then use our thinking to back up those immediate judgements.

Code 2/1 insists on a systematic scan. First there are the 'plus' or positive points. The thinker makes an effort to look in this direction even if he or she does not like the idea.

Next comes the effort to look in the 'minus' or negative direction. What are the faults? What are the problems? What might go wrong? Even if you are enthusiastic about the idea you still make an honest effort to see the difficulties. Often you get a big surprise.

Finally you look in the 'interesting' direction. These are points that are

CODE 2

2/1

neither good nor bad. They are interesting. They are worth noting. They are worth speculating about.

Code 2/1 is a request to carry out the complete scan and to report back on what has been perceived. Research shows over and over again that such a formal scan often reverses judgements and choices.

It requires a considerable discipline and mental effort to carry out a systematic scan when you already know that you like, or dislike, the idea.

What is extraordinary about these attention-directing tools is that they are so very simple but can be very powerful. That is because attention normally 'flows' from one point of interest to another. The mind is reluctant to perform a systematic scan – unless asked to do so.

2/2 Direct your attention to the future.
What might be the immediate consequences?
What might be the short-term consequences?
What might be the medium-term
consequences? And the long-term
consequences? This is another systematic scan.
Report what you see.

Code 2/2 is equivalent to the C&S tool in CoRT and DATT. It stands for 'consequences and sequel'. This was the tool which the women executives were asked to use. When they systematically considered the consequences of women being paid 15 per cent more than men for the same job, they mostly changed their approval of the idea to disapproval.

The interesting point is that most of the executives would have claimed that they always looked at the consequences of a change. To some extent I am sure they did. But being asked to scan the future systematically is very different.

It is characteristic of these attention-directing tools that people claim to use them all the time. Yet when they are asked to scan systematically and formally the results are very different.

Having the general intention of doing something is not at all the same as doing that thing formally and deliberately.

CODE 2

2/3 *What are the factors involved here? What factors do we have to think about? What things do we have to consider? What is relevant here? Please scan for the factors that ought to be considered.*

This request is the equivalent of the CAF (Consider All Factors) attention-directing tool in the CoRT and DATT programmes.

If you are designing a chair what factors should you consider?

If you are making an investment what factors should you consider?

If you are employing someone, what factors should be considered?

If you are planning a summer holiday, what factors should be considered?

If you are buying a pair of shoes, what factors should be considered?

Code 2/3 is very broad and comes into most thinking. Code 2/3 is a general scan around to see what should be seen.

In a sense code 2/3 is open-ended. You can always add to the list of factors that should be considered. There are the central or important factors and then there may be outer or remote factors that might, just possibly, be worth considering. There needs to be a practical cut-off.

As with the other attention-directing codes, there is a natural tendency to rush ahead with a plan or course of action without really considering all the factors. That is why this artificial instruction may be so useful.

CODE 2

2/3

Different people may have different ideas of what factors should be considered. This may depend on experience, values or objectives. There is no one right answer. The code encourages 'an effort' to seek out factors which need to be considered.

CODE 2

2/4 What is the objective? What is the goal? What are we really trying to do? What are we aiming for?

Code 2/4 is equivalent to the AGO (Aims, Goals, Objectives) in both the CoRT and DATT programmes.

It is surprising how vague and poorly defined an objective may become. Or the objective may be clear at the beginning but then the momentum of the action takes over. Each next step is determined by the previous step. The original objective is blurred or even forgotten.

So code 2/4 is a request to focus again on the purpose of the thinking or action. What is to be achieved? There may be a broad objective and then more specific sub-objectives.

A defined value may be the objective, in which case the means to deliver that value are then sought.

It may be useful to ask: Why are we doing this? The same question is then asked of the answer – and so on. Sometimes, this can be carried too far with the ultimate question: Why are we alive?

CODE 2

2/5 What are the views of the other people involved? What might be the thinking of the other people involved?

Code 2/5 is equivalent to the OPV (Other People's Views) tool in both CoRT and DATT. This is a very important attention-directing tool.

At school, problems are abstract and real people are never involved. In life, however, real people are involved in almost any thinking that is taking place. Code 2/5 is a formal request to consider all these other people. What are their views? What are their values? What are their thoughts?

The first part of the process is to identify the other people involved. Who are they? The second part of the process is to seek 'to get into the shoes of the other people' and see the world through their eyes.

There is some overlap with code 2/3 because other people are factors that need to be considered. Because other people are so important they also deserve a special attention-directing tool.

There may be people who are very directly involved: like two taxi drivers in an argument. There are then people who are less directly involved: like the passengers in the taxis and other motorists trying to get by. Less directly involved are bystanders and the taxi owners. The police become involved if they are called.

The use of code 2/5 (as the OPV tool) has dissolved many conflicts. Once each party makes the effort to see the thinking of the other party, then the conflict evaporates.

It may be noted that code 2/5 is very similar to code 6/2 (of the frantic

CODE 2

2/5

code). The exchange of views is like a particular type of code 2/5. There is no problem with such an overlap. Under certain circumstances different codes may achieve similar results.

CODE 2

2/6 What are the alternatives? What are the alternative ways of looking at this? What are the alternative courses of action? What are the options? What are the possibilities?

This is a direct request for creative thinking. There is a deliberate effort to find alternatives.

The most probable explanation immediately comes to mind. What are other possible explanations? A course of action immediately comes to mind. What are other possible courses of action?

There seem to be a limited number of choices. What are the other possible choices?

Code 2/6 is a deliberate request to go 'beyond the obvious'. Code 2/6 is concerned with 'possibilities'. Once you can think of a possibility, then you can explore that possibility to determine its values.

Code 2/6 corresponds to the APC tool in the CoRT and DATT programmes. It is an instruction to make a creative effort.

CODE 2

2/7 What are the priorities? Which things matter the most? What is really important here? Which things have to come first?

Code 2/7 corresponds to the FIP tool in the CoRT and DATT programmes: First Important Priorities.

Many of the attention-directing tools can produce a long list of items. For example code 2/3 can produce a long list of factors to be considered. Code 2/2 may produce a long list of possible consequences. There is a need to recognize that not all the items on these long lists are equally important. So code 2/7 is a request to select the most important items from a list – or in general. What matters most?

In any situation it may sometimes be useful to define the priorities up front. This can give more direction to the thinking that follows. Decisions and choices are heavily dependent on priorities: what are the important values?

There are some things which need to be done 'first' even though they are not otherwise important. The contents of a letter may be very important. Putting a stamp on the letter and finding a postbox are not important – but they have to be done first. There is a sort of 'gateway' effect. If you cannot get through the gate then nothing else matters.

Compared to the rest of your home the key to the front door is trivial. But if you cannot open the front door then nothing else matters.

Code 2/7 is an assessment code: what matters most? There may well be disagreements as to the priorities. Such disagreements can be discussed and sorted out. The important point is that attention has been directed at priorities.

CODE 2

2/8 Direct your attention to the key values involved. What are the values here? What are the key values? Identify the key values.

This attention-directing tool is equivalent to the KVI (Key Values Involved) tool in the DATT programme.

In the end, all thinking and behaviour is about values. Just as there is a need to be very clear about objectives, so also there is a need to be very clear about values. It is not enough to have a vague, fuzzy sense of values. It should be possible to spell out the key values in a clear way and at any moment. That is the purpose of the code.

The word 'key' is included because there may be many values. Some of these values will be central but others will be peripheral. So the focus is on the central and key values.

In any situation there will be different values for different people so there is an element of code 2/5 (other people's thinking). There is no need to state this other code since other people's values are part of the code 2/8 process. As before, overlap is not a problem.

There are values involved in why we choose things and why we make decisions. There are values involved in designing anything. There are values involved in solving problems.

There are not only the values of those doing the thinking, but also the values of those who will be affected by the thinking. How will this proposal be received? Is this solution acceptable?

CODE 2

2/8

There are the obvious values such as money, benefits, prestige, etc. There is also a need to look for less obvious values such as simplicity, convenience, security, status, etc.

In looking for values it is essential to look also for 'negative values'. This may seen a contradiction in terms but it is important. Insecurity is a negative value. 'Loss of face' is a negative value. Anxiety and stress are negative values. The value scan needs to pay as much attention to negative values (to be avoided) as to positive values (to be delivered).

A value scan is an important part of all thinking that is not purely abstract.

CODE 2

2/9 *Direct your attention to the matters on which we agree. Direct your attention to the matters on which we disagree. Separate out the matters which are really irrelevant to the issue.*

In any negotiation or dispute situation this sort of attention directing can be a big help. Code 2/9 comes into the third section of the CoRT programme as ADI (Agree, Disagree, Irrelevant).

In many disputes it often turns out that there is really a lot of agreement. The points of disagreement are important but minor compared to the agreed points.

Directing attention to the points of disagreement allows those specific matters to be dealt with. It now becomes easier to design a way forward which can satisfy both parties.

In disputes it may often seem that the people involved are in total disagreement and conflict over all matters. Code 2/9 can give a much clearer picture.

In disputes it is neither normal nor usual for the parties to spell out the points of agreement. Code 2/9 provides a specific mechanism which allows either party to request this scan.

It often turns out that many points that are being argued about are really 'irrelevant' and can therefore be ignored. The code 2/9 scan can make it clear which points are irrelevant and not important in the dispute.

CODE 2

2/9

Both sides in a dispute should lay out the points they see under each of the scan stages: what is agreed; what is not agreed; and what is irrelevant. There may not be full agreement on these points but at least they can be discussed.

CODE 2

2/10 *Can you recognize this as a standard situation? How would you analyse this? Can we divide this up to make it easier to think about?*

The purpose of code 2/10 is to make the thinking easier. It corresponds to RAD (Recognize, Analyse, Divide) in the DATT programme.

If you can recognize something as a standard situation then you may know the standard response. This is like a doctor diagnosing an illness and applying the standard treatment.

You may wish to think beyond the standard response to a standard situation. But at least you know it is there as a fall-back position.

If something is not immediately recognizable then there is a need to analyse the situation to see if the components are recognizable. The analysis effort seeks to break down the situation into its real components. What things have come together to cause this situation?

The 'divide' element is quite different from analysis. Analysis seeks to identify the true components. 'Divide' seeks to divide up a situation into 'arbitrary' chunks. These chunks are chosen for convenience. The situation is broken down into 'bite-sized' pieces so it can be digested more easily.

The chosen divisions help the thinker or thinkers to direct attention to one part after another instead of just thinking about the whole. The distinction between 'analyse' and 'divide' is an important one. At any moment it is useful to be clear about what is being done.

ACTION CODE
CODE 3

As the name implies the 'action' code is quick, sharp and definite.

The situations are not as complex as with some of the other codes. The advantage of the code is the clarity with which the communication can be made. There is no room for ambiguity.

The action code can be used in any type of situation, whether personal or business. If the code seems suitable to express an intention, then use it.

At certain points there may be an overlap with some other codes. This does not matter. Sometimes it is possible to express the same thing in various ways ('top of the mountain', 'peak', 'summit', etc.).

The code may be used in conjunction with other codes to add a further layer of meaning.

Code 3
Action Code

3/1 *I want in. I want to take part in this. I want to be included. I like this. I want to join the team or group or project.*

The code signals a firm wish to take part in whatever is specified. The code is simple, clear and unambiguous.

It may be an investment opportunity or a planned outing. The decision has been made.

Note that 3/1 goes beyond 'interest'. Code 3/1 is not suggesting that negotiations begin. Code 3/1 is a definite acceptance of the situation and a desire to become part of the action. The conditions are those that have already been spelled out or made apparent.

CODE 3

3/2 I am very interested. Tell me more. Explain the situation in more detail. How is it going to be done? How is it going to work?

This is a definite communication of interest but falls short of the commitment shown in 3/1.

The point of the code is to show definite interest with a view to assessing the situation more clearly. The results of this assessment may be a commitment to join – or it may not.

A specific request for information may be made in addition to this demonstration of 'interest'. There may be a need for more information in general or on certain aspects.

'I am interested. I would like to explore this further.'
'I am interested. What do I need to know?'

3/3 *Thank you, but no thank you. I am not interested. Count me out. I do not want to join. I do not want to take part in this.*

This is as firm a rejection as 3/1 is an acceptance.

There is no need to specify the reasons for the rejection, although they may be asked for. There may be some specific point of difficulty or the project as a whole is not interesting.

Just as a person is assumed innocent until proved guilty so a project is uninteresting until shown to be interesting.

Code 3/3 suggests that the decision has been made and that there is no point in pursuing the matter further.

CODE 3

3/4 I want out. I want to get out of this. I do not want to be involved in this any more.

In this case the person is already involved but makes it clear that he or she or the organization wants to get out of the involvement.

Code 3/4 would not usually be followed by reasons. The matter is not open to negotiation. The decision has been made.

In the 'quick code' the thinking has usually taken place already and it is the result of the thinking that is being communicated. It is a 'decision' code.

CODE 3

3/5 Let's move right forward to action. Let's get going. What are we waiting for? Action!

This is a direct call for immediate action. The car needs to be put on the road. The project should be moved forward.

It is assumed that the direction of the action and the necessary steps have already been decided upon. Code 3/5 is not a call for random action.

'The time for consideration is over. Let's move forward into action.'

'Action time. What do we do first?'

CODE 3

3/6 What is the problem? What is the hold-up? Why are we not moving forward?

The decision has been made but the action is not moving forward smoothly. Why? What is the obstacle?

Code 3/6 is a request for a report on the problem. If the problem has not yet been identified then it is a call to identify the problem.

There may be one major problem, or a lot of smaller problems, or just poor management. Somewhere there is a reason why things are not proceeding as they should. What is that reason?

There is an element of impatience in code 3/6.

3/7 *We need to design a way forward. We need to solve the problem. We need to find a way around the problem. So let's do that.*

Some problems can be solved by finding and then removing the cause of the problem. In other cases you may need to design a way forward, leaving the problem in place.

Even where there are no problems as such, there may be a need to design a way forward if this is not obvious.

Designing a way forward may also apply to negotiations – as will be seen in the negotiation code. Designing is a matter of putting together what we have in order to achieve what we want.

This design request may be made at the beginning of the project with a need to design an action plan.

CODE 3

3/8 We need some creative thinking here. We need some new ideas. Can we try a different approach?

This direct request for creative thinking also comes into other codes.

There is a realization that matters cannot proceed unless there is a new approach. As a result there is a direct request for deliberate creative thinking.

Creative thinking is not something that just happens. Creative thinking can be worked on formally and deliberately (as with lateral thinking).

Creative thinking should not have to 'force' its way into the discussion. The door should be open. Once there is an acknowledged need for new ideas (signalled by 3/8) then there is an effort to produce such new ideas.

CODE 3

3/9 There seems to be an energy failure. There are no problems but nothing seems to be happening. Why is that?

It may be a failure of motivation. It may be a failure of energy. It may be a shortage of resources. It may be due to a distraction of attention. There can be many reasons why something is not moving forward even when there are no problems in the way.

Code 3/9 wants to know why things are not moving forward as intended.

The answer may be simple or it may be vague if a lot of small factors are involved.

The main point about 3/9 is that it is not asking about problems but about the 'lack of energy' in a project. It could be called the 'laziness' of the project.

CODE 3

3/10 *What is the immediate next step?*
What do you do next? What do we do next?
What should be done next? What needs to be
done next?

The emphasis is on the very next step. A journey of a thousand miles has to proceed with the next step. Along that journey the next step is needed if progress is to be made.

The next step may be known. The next step may need clarifying. The next step may need designing.

CODE 3

3/11 *We need to think about this. Some thinking is needed at this point. Action needs to be interrupted by some thinking.*

The thinking that is suggested may be 'joint' thinking or someone may be asked to go away to think and come back with some answers.

Things may not be going smoothly. Circumstances may have changed. For whatever reason there seems to be a need for thinking instead of just reacting to a new situation.

There is a need for 'time out' to think. It is possible to go down a track, taking one step after another and doing no more thinking than is required for the next step. There are times, however, when it is useful to step back to consider a picture that is broader than the very next step.

So there is thinking to overcome difficulties and thinking to review the direction. Both can be requested with this code.

3/12 What has been happening? What is the feedback? Where is the action report?

The action has been taking place and is being monitored. The request is for information on progress. How are things doing? What has been achieved? What stage has been reached?

The request is a simple and direct request for a report on the action. Once the general report has been obtained then specific questions can be asked in addition.

'Tell me what is going on.'

DIFFICULT SITUATIONS
CODE 4

Few situations are ideal. Some are more difficult than others. There are times when it is necessary to work in a difficult situation.

Code 4 is an attempt to categorize some difficult situations in order to be able to recognize them more clearly – and even to do something about them.

This code is as much for recognition and reference as for communication. Complaining about a difficult situation does not necessarily make it better.

The code may be used when describing different environments – this can be the communication value.

There are many aspects of 'difficult' and only some of them are included here.

Code 4
Difficult Situations

4/1 Lack of the necessary resources. Certain things which are needed for the job in hand are simply not available.

There may be a lack of money. There may be a lack of skilled labour. There may be a lack of raw materials. There may be a lack of equipment. There may be a lack of transport or communication facilities.

The lack of resources may be general, as in some developing countries. Or the lack may be specific. For example, the lack of IT-trained people, even in a highly developed country.

Teachers in school may lack teaching materials. Hospitals may lack basic pharmaceuticals or even nurses.

It is not difficult to pinpoint situations where there is a manifest lack of resources for what needs to be done.

It is possible to have a 'wish list' of resources which is far in excess of what is really fundamental. This may be nice but unrealistic. At the same time there is a baseline below which resources should not fall.

Missionaries used to make do with very scarce resources and ingenuity can do the same. Nevertheless, a serious lack of resources makes for a very difficult environment.

4/2 Lack of management at all levels or at some levels.

Management could have been classed as a 'resource' but lack of management is so important that it deserves a code of its own.

If there is good management then lack of resources is less of a problem. But if there is poor management lack of resources becomes an even bigger problem.

There are times when the senior management is excellent but there is a real lack at 'sergeant' or NCO level. There may also be a lack at supervisory level.

Good management may be a matter of personality, education, experience and culture. Training can work wonders and it may be the lack of this which is easiest to put right.

It may, of course, be a situation in which there could be good managers but those who have got into power are not the good managers. They may be there for family reasons in a family firm. They may be there for political reasons, etc.

Code 4/2 does not always mean that good managers are not available, but only that they are not in position.

CODE 4

4/3 *Low morale. Low motivation. A workforce uninterested in what they are doing.*

Such situations may arise from poor management or from a variety of other reasons. The recruitment policy may be responsible.

People do the job in front of them just well enough to get by. There is no motivation to do it better. It is enough to survive to the next day.

There was a time when many public-service departments might have seen themselves under this coding. Things have changed and are changing due to better leadership.

Poor morale is contagious because once it has been established newcomers soon pick up the local culture. If they do not, then they have a hard time with their workmates.

CODE 4

4/4 Lack of leadership.

Some organizations seek to avoid dependence on a good leader. Such organizations prefer to have things set up so they function well no matter what leadership is in place.

Leadership gets a lot of attention but remains ill-defined. The leader sets the mood. The leader sets the vision. The leader sets the values and culture. The leader raises morale.

Most people's image of their house is of the façade. In the same way a large part of the image of an organization is based on the leader.

Excellent leaders have been credited with turning around even large organizations. This is partly based on making the right decisions but even more on inspiring others to make the right decisions.

Most people in an organization with poor leadership know it. They also know it if there is excellent leadership. In between is the grey area of leadership which is neither very bad nor exceptionally good.

It is also very convenient to blame all woes on poor leadership. This can become fashionable.

CODE 4

4/5 *An organization that is rigid and old-fashioned. An organization that is not interested in change and has got left behind. Everything is done by a rule book that has not been changed for a very long time.*

There are organizations that are 'dead' but still functioning. Lack of competition allows such organizations to keep going.

In such organizations change is seen as both unnecessary and disruptive. Things have always been done in a certain way – so why change them?

Such organizations pride themselves on avoiding the latest management fads and fancies.

Surprisingly, such organizations do reasonably well right up to the point when they collapse. This is like jumping off the top of a tall building and saying 'so far, so good' all the way down.

CODE 4

4/6 Lack of vision. Lack of mission. Survival is enough.

A job is a job and provides income. An organization is a collection of people with jobs. Who needs a vision? Few organizations would admit to thinking that way – but they may behave exactly as if they were thinking that way.

There is no destination to be reached, no goal. Each step repeats the ones that have gone before.

No one in the organization notices this lack of vision because that is their normality.

There is no need to improve or get better because 'adequate' is always good enough. Energy without a destination is wasted energy.

CODE 4

4/7 *The world outside is tough. The environment is difficult. Everything takes time and a great deal of effort. Life is not easy.*

There are environments which are very tough no matter how well run the organization itself may be.

There may be political instability and physical danger. Everything takes time and requires 'special' permits.

Tasks which in other countries would be routine become major under-takings.

Even the climate may not be very helpful.

There are environments which on any objective measurement are tough to live in and to work in. The effort is on adjustment and finding how to get things done.

CODE 4

4/8 Situations which are 'locked' in. The best motivation in the world will not help systems that are designed to prevent change.

The education system in most countries is a prime example of a 'locked in' system.

The subjects taught are largely out of date and are only there because they were there yesterday and the day before. There are much more important and relevant subjects which are not taught at all.

The system is often tied in to examinations set by universities for their own purposes. Teachers have to do what they are supposed to do – otherwise the parents will be upset.

In my experience there is a huge amount of talent, experience and motivation in the education system – but it gets nowhere because the system is locked in.

Some belief systems are 'locked in'. The belief system tells you to look at the world in a certain way. That certain way reinforces the belief system itself.

Organizations that choose problem solvers as chief executives find themselves short on strategy.

Universities select staff who will perpetuate the 'scholarship' mode when the world is crying out for the 'design' mode.

CODE 4

4/9 Fights, factions, disputes and far too much internal politics. Not a peaceful place in which to get on with the work that needs to be done.

Some people like fights. Some cultures encourage fights and suggest that if you do not take part in the politics you will be left behind.

People in such organizations come to spend most of their mental energy and a considerable amount of time in disputes and political jockeying.

To people in such an organization it seems normal. Are not all organizations like this? A newcomer from a more tranquil organization notices the difference at once.

The tranquil spires of academia and even the peace of a convent often contain fierce bickerings and jealousies.

CODE 4

4/10 *Too much corruption, cheating, nepotism, etc. An organization with rather low morals.*

Even though the accusation may seem rather extreme, such organizations do exist. Little by little, there is more and more that you can 'get away with'.

From time to time the press reveals that a particular police force is alleged to be corrupt. What is surprising is how quickly unusual behaviour gets to become routine and accepted. Whistle-blowers usually have a hard time being believed.

CODE 4

4/11 Coasting. A once-successful organization, group or even country coasts on its reputation.

Success breeds culture and confidence. Satisfaction with the past may leave no room for designing the future. Surely the future will be 'more of the same'?

Once-powerful organizations get left behind when technology or the environment changes.

The Xerox corporation designed many of the most-used processes in computing. Xerox could have taken the lead as a computer company. But success had been built on renting out copiers, so little time was given to the computer developments from their own research park.

Leaders fail when their sense of style becomes so strong that they no longer consider the situation but say to themselves, 'What would Maggie Thatcher do here?'

It is perfectly possible to be trapped by the successes of the past.

RESPONSE CODE
CODE 5

There is some overlap between the 'response code' and the 'pre-code' (code 1). The response code is specifically concerned with responses. There may be no communication, text or message following the response code – so it can hardly be a 'pre' code.

The response code is the shortest possible way of responding to a communication or request – short of simply ignoring the request.

Where the recipient may not know the code, it may be necessary to send a code sheet or even have the code printed on the back of letterheads (under licence).

The response code saves time and energy for both parties. It also makes clear exactly what the position is.

There are two basic types of request. There are requests from people who have every right to make a request. Then there are requests from people who are not part of the organization, framework, structure, etc., but who want to make a request.

Codes used for responses may seem impolite but if they convey the necessary information they serve the purpose well enough. There is no reason why communication politeness should be long-winded.

The code could be added to the original letter or fax, which is then returned to the sender.

Code 5
Response Code

5/1 I am sorry, this matter is not of interest to me. Thank you for sending it. It may be worthwhile but I cannot comment on it.

Some people get material sent to them for their comments. The matter may be very important to the sender but is outside the receiver's area of expertise. There has to be a simple way of indicating this.

There are also times when the receiver does not want to get into a discussion on an issue. This may be a matter of pressure of time. Code 5/1 is a simple and direct way of declining to show interest.

It could be said that code 5/1 is unnecessary since a simple failure to reply would serve the same purpose. But a person who has communicated something that is of importance to him or her probably deserves some sort of reply.

CODE 5

5/2 *Here is the information that you wanted.*

The information that has been requested is now presented. This particular code is very similar to a pre-code.

The precise information requested is then sent with this code.

This code should only be used if the full information requested can be sent. If not, one of the other codes may be more suitable.

CODE 5

5/3 This is some of the information that you requested. I am not able to supply the rest of it.

This is the code to use when the reply partially satisfies the request.

Information may be given as to where the missing information might be obtained.

If the information supplied is of doubtful value then this should be indicated.

If most of the information requested cannot be supplied it is best to indicate this with another code.

CODE 5

5/4 *I am not able to provide you with the information that you requested. If I have any suggestions as to where you may get the information I shall add this. If there are no such suggestions it means I do not know where you could get the information.*

This code indicates that the information simply cannot be supplied. If the person who has received the request does have some useful suggestions these could be added. At the same time, some people are really too busy to be used as information sources.

It is easy enough to ask for information, but it does put a burden of activity on whoever is asked.

Code 5/4 will be used in different ways by different people. There are some people whose job it is to supply information and others to whom the business of supplying information is an interruption.

CODE 5

5/5 You are asking for far too much
information. To give you all the information
you requested would take a great deal of
time and effort. Unfortunately I do not have
the time.

Some people ask for a blanket amount of information: 'Give me information on all the workers in the field of creativity over the last fifty years.'

The request may be innocent in that the asker may simply have no idea as
to how much information is being requested. There are, however, those
who need to collect information themselves and are happy to pass that
task over to someone else.

'Tell me all the goods you carry in your supermarket.' It is easy enough to
communicate such a request but rather more trouble to respond to it.

Code 5/5 does carry a slight rebuke to those who ask for 'everything'.

CODE 5

5/6 *I could be interested in what you have suggested but I would need much more information (which may be indicated by the questions). In particular I would like you to spell out the benefits.*

Specific questions may then be posed. These need to be as focused as possible. It is best to cover all areas at the beginning rather than keep on going to and fro for further information.

'I am interested. But convince me that I should take it further.' The person sending the communication is given the task of showing why the matter should be pursued further.

In some cases it may even be dangerous to show this slight amount of interest. This may be followed by an avalanche of information, phone calls, e-mails, etc.

So code 5/6 should never be used simply out of politeness. Unless the 'interest' is genuine it may be best not to show any interest at all.

CODE 5

5/7 I am going to have to think about this matter and will then get back to you. I may need reminding.

This code should not be used as a 'holding' code. Unless there is a genuine intention to think about the matter, there is no point in indicating this.

The reminder part may be necessary, as matters that once seemed important later get submerged by other matters.

This code is not intended as a version of: 'Don't call me, I'll call you.' That response is so obviously a rejection that it is better to decline interest honestly and directly.

5/8 Thank you for your proposal. Here are my reactions to your proposal. There may also be amendments to your proposal or even a counter-proposal.

There is little point in having three separate codes for reaction, amendment and counter-proposal. The response to a proposal may take one of several possible forms.

A delay in responding to the proposal is also a form of response. Code 5/8 can be used and a 'delay' indicated.

5/9 *With regard to your suggestion of a meeting I would like to have in writing what you would wish to discuss at such a meeting. Please let me know why you want this meeting.*

There does not always need to be a specific reason for a meeting. The meeting can be semi-social. If so, this can be stated. The reason why the recipient of the suggestion to meet should agree to that meeting needs to be suggested: 'I want to tell you about my experiences in teaching thinking to very young children.'

Where there is a specific reason for the meeting it should be spelled out. If the reason is good this may increase the possibility of the meeting taking place. There are always some 'crazies' who want a meeting for no particular reason.

Someone who wants your time and attention should indicate the reason for the request.

5/10 *Thank you very much for your comments. They are much appreciated. I am afraid I do not have time to reply in more detail but I do want to thank you for taking the trouble to communicate with me.*

Code 5/10 is an appreciation of an appreciation. If someone has bothered to send in an appreciation then that should be appreciated.

Thank you for your kind comments. Thank you for your good wishes. Thank you for your observations.

It is often as difficult to be appreciative of nice comments as it is unusual to make them. There is the intention to thank but words seem limited. The code makes the intention clear.

CODE 5

5/11 *I accept your invitation and will be happy to be there.*

A simple acceptance of an invitation or suggestion. The code could be appended to the card or invitation itself. Otherwise the date and occasion also need specifying.

CODE 5

5/12 *I regret that I am unable to accept your invitation owing to a prior engagement. Thank you for asking me.*

Simplified regrets at being unable to accept an invitation. What interests the person issuing the invitation is whether it is accepted or not. The reasons are unimportant since they may or may not be valid. A quick reply is more valuable than a slow but flowery one.

CODE 5

5/13 *I am sure you are entitled to your opinion no matter how you arrived at it.*

Bad-tempered communications could well be ignored or code 5/13 could be used to acknowledge the communication without starting a correspondence or argument. Many people send such communications in order to get attention and in order to draw the recipient into an argument.

INTERACTION (FRANTIC) CODE 6

The story goes that President Yeltsin and President Clinton were having an intense private discussion in the Kremlin. Suddenly a frantic figure bursts in. He identifies himself as the Minister of Finance.

'President Yeltsin, I need your attention immediately. We have a big problem with the IMF. There is a need for immediate action.'

President Yeltsin waves his arm and says: 'Code 6.'

Immediately the man calms down and walks out.

A while later another frantic person breaks in. He identifies himself as the Foreign Minister.

'President Yeltsin, we have a crisis with the Islamic nations. This will affect our southern areas. There is a need for an immediate discussion. This is urgent.'

President Yeltsin waves his arm and says: 'Code 6.'

The man calms down and leaves.

President Clinton is very impressed and asks what 'Code 6' might be. Yeltsin tells him: 'It simply means don't take yourself so seriously.'

Sometimes in frantic situations there is a need for a quick and unambiguous signal that can defuse the situation. So code 6 is built around the above joke.

There are things which are difficult to say directly because they are personal and may seem offensive. Having a neutral code gets over this difficulty.

The code also covers more complexity than can be described in a word or two.

The codes can also be used in a light-hearted way – and still convey the meaning powerfully.

108

Code 6
Interaction (Frantic)
Code

6/1 What exactly is the matter? Spell out the problem directly and simply. Summarize what it is all about.

This is a direct request that the other person (the frantic one) should state the situation or problem as clearly and simply as possible.

There should be no build-up, background, perspective, etc. Just get to the point. Lay out the difficulty or problem.

What is it that needs this urgent attention?

It is not always easy to state what the problem is. You may focus on the underlying reasons or on the effects, rather than on the situation itself.

Is the problem that the bath in the apartment upstairs is overflowing? Is it that water is pouring through the ceiling? Is it that the carpet, papers and valuable furniture may be damaged?

If there is something which requires the frantic communication, then that something needs to be spelled out precisely.

CODE 6

If there is a dispute then the fundamental cause of the dispute needs to be spelled out. What exactly is the matter? What are you upset about? What has gone wrong? What is the problem?

CODE 6

6/2 You give me what you think my point of view might be and I shall give you what I think your point of view might be.

In the CoRT Thinking Lessons there is an attention-directing tool called OPV. This means focusing on the other person's view. It means seeking to stand in the shoes of the other person to see what that person might be thinking.

This code is particularly useful when a conflict is building up (the process of 'confliction') or where a conflict is actually in progress.

Once you can see what the other person perceives you can correct any misperceptions. In the same way, when you make an effort to see things from the other party's point of view, then it becomes easier to design a way forward out of the conflict.

Instead of each party just pushing their own point of view and sense of grievance, there is now an effort to understand the other party.

In practice the OPV has solved many disputes and fights.

CODE 6

6/3 *There are things we do need to discuss here. Let us find time to discuss them. It need not be right now.*

This code is an acknowledgement that there are matters that need to be talked over and talked through. If possible, this should be in a calmer state of mind rather than the frantic one of the present moment. Occasionally the urgency of the situation may demand immediate consideration but this is not usually the case.

In a sense code 6/3 is a promise to find time to discuss matters. It is not just a way of defusing the difficulties of the moment.

It may be that some temporary action is required; the underlying problem can then be considered more carefully at a later time.

The important point about 6/3 is that it is an acknowledgement that there are matters which do need discussing.

CODE 6

__6/4__ Give me space. Don't crowd me. Don't pressure me. Don't keep going on at me. Back off.

This is a signal that the person making the signal feels that he or she is being pressured, harried, harassed, etc.

The pressure is seen to be quite separate from the issue itself. The pressure is a matter of behaviour and perhaps of overreaction.

The code is not a dismissal of the matter or the person. It is a suggestion or a request that the matter be dealt with in a less 'pressurizing' way.

Sometimes people are not even aware that they are 'pressuring' other people. So the code points this out to them. It is not so much an accusation as an 'awareness prompt'.

6/5 *Calm down. There is no need to be frantic or aggressive. There is no point in fighting about this. We can discuss it and work things out.*

Too often conflicts are fed in a positive feedback way. Aggression in one party excites 'defensive' aggression in the other party. So matters escalate into a conflict even though neither party believes that the conflict mode will solve anything.

6/5 is a sort of 'time-out' mechanism or safety valve. It is a suggestion from one party that the conflict mode is neither essential nor very constructive.

Once the codes are in common use both parties will want to be the first to suggest code 6/5.

It may be that the other party will refuse to respond to the code signal. That is always possible with any means of 'de-confliction'. If there is no response the code will have been used in vain. This is no great loss. The signal has been given.

CODE 6

6/6 *Don't take yourself so seriously. Don't overreact. It is not the end of the world. Take a broader perspective. Don't be so frantic. Things can be worked out.*

There is always the background sense that the person who is taking himself or herself so seriously is being rather ridiculous. This is not a direct part of the code but is an implication of it.

The main signal indicates that the overreaction is unnecessary and probably unproductive.

CODE 6

6/7 Cut the crap, what do you want? Never mind the preamble and background, what is it that you actually want?

This code has some similarity to code 6/1 but the key difference is the focus on 'want'. What do you want? What do you want to happen? What do you want from me?

It may be permission that is needed. It may be advice that is needed. It may be a new idea that is needed. It may be resources that are needed.

The code asks the direct question: What is it that you want?

It may even be that what the person wants is that you help that person decide what is really needed!

CODE 6

6/8 *Things are becoming too emotional. I suggest we take a break. We can discuss the matter later in a calmer atmosphere. The thinking at the moment would be too much influenced by emotional factors.*

It is not so much an accusation that the other party has become too emotional as an admission that the 'situation' is becoming too driven by emotion.

The suggestion is for a postponement of the matter. The matter is indeed to be discussed, but at a later date.

There is some overlap with 6/3 in the sense that a future discussion is promised. The emphasis, however, is on the emotional aspects which would prevent a reasoned consideration of the matter.

It is important to accept that the code is not an 'accusation' (even where this might be justified) but an acknowledgement that an emotional atmosphere is making the situation more difficult.

INFORMATION CODE
CODE 7

Technology is rapidly creating a situation of information overload. On the Net there are so many references to my work that if you spent just two minutes on each reference it would take you sixty working years (9 a.m. to 5 p.m., five days a week) to access them all.

There are people who receive so many e-mails that they have little time for anything else. Matters will only get worse.

There is a huge need for some way of classifying information so that the receiver or searcher can tell, at once, its nature and value.

So an information code is part of the de Bono code. This code is put forward here. There is a huge need for it, especially on the Internet.

It may be argued that people will cheat and misuse the code in order to get more attention for their information. This is always a possibility. But sources that cheat will get such a bad reputation that all their information will be devalued and ignored. The word will spread that certain sources can be disregarded because of the dishonest classification of their information.

The information code indicates the type of information that follows the coding. The code does not guarantee the value or accuracy of that information.

The value of the code is that at a glance you can tell the nature of the information. Is it factual? Is it an opinion? Is it advocacy? Is it comprehensive?

CODE 7

If you want to book a flight you want factual information. If you want to choose a hotel for your holiday you may want a subjective opinion as well as factual information.

Code 7
Information Code

7/1 This information is purely factual. It is comprehensive and not selective. No interpretation of the information is given.

An example of 7/1 might be a train timetable or an airline schedule. The facts are laid out. There is no attempt to suggest the best train or plane.

Meteorological data over the last ten years (temperature, rainfall, etc.) would be another example of factual information. So would be statistics on road deaths, population distribution, budget allocation, etc.

The analysis of a soil sample is factual but it also depends on what was tested. There may be important things that were left out. It would come under 7/1 with a caution regarding the thoroughness of the tests.

Tax levels and hourly wage rates in different countries would be factual and objective – provided the countries were not selected to prove some point.

In theory, 7/1 indicates the most objective, the most neutral and the most factual display of information. The caution that should be kept in mind is: how comprehensive is this?

A stockbroker may give entirely factual information on the period when his services provided his customers with profits – but may leave out the loss-making years.

120

CODE 7

Directories, indexes, etc., obviously come under 7/1.

A request for information using the pre-code 1/2 may specify the information needed as 7/1.

CODE 7

7/2 *These are administrative details. They are contact details, addresses, e-mail addresses, telephone numbers, etc.*

In a way this factual information could be a subset of 7/1, but there is value in having it separately so that you can look for and identify the place where this precise type of information is given.

For the sake of simplicity, operational procedures may also be included under 7/2. For example, information on how to purchase goods may be given at the same time as the contact address. How to make a plane reservation over the phone might accompany the airline schedule.

In general, however, instructions and operating procedures would fit more easily under code 7/3.

CODE 7

7/3 Instructions, operating procedures, laws, regulations, etc.

These are factual in themselves but need to be understood and applied.

The recipes in a cookbook would come under 7/3. There is no guarantee that they would work or that you could carry them out. But they are factual operating instructions.

The key characteristic of code 7/3 is that the instructions or laws are set out as facts. How they are applied or even whether they work is another matter.

CODE 7

7/4 *This information is intended to be an honest, objective description of or comment on some matter. At the same time, it is an individual who is doing the describing.*

7/4 implies an attempt at honest and objective description, but may still contain a subjective element.

The person who writes the geography textbook used in schools is indeed seeking to be objective and honest and may perform well in this respect.

There is, however, a significant difference between an airline schedule and someone's description of the geography of a country. There is always the matter of subjective selection and emphasis. Which matters get most attention? What gets left out?

The important point about 7/4 is that it does seem to be an honest attempt at objectivity.

CODE 7

7/5 *This is a subjective category, description or review. The personality of the person making the commentary is an important ingredient.*

The commentator is not seeking to be dishonest or prejudiced or to make a case; the view is nevertheless subjective.

While the writer of a geography textbook may succeed in being objective, the writer of a history textbook may not. There has to be speculation about connections, influences and causes and effects. So the ultimate result is much more personal. The same applies to a sports commentator.

A reviewer of films or books is in the same position. There may be an attempt at honest objectivity but the result is still subjective and is intended to be subjective. An art critic is in the same position.

CODE 7

7/6 *This is a dishonest review or commentary; the reviewer is starting off with some prejudice and not really seeking to describe the material at all.*

This happens quite often. The prejudice may be based on jealousy (usually the case) or some dislike of the person who has produced the music, the film or the book.

All reviews are by their nature subjective, but are meant to be based on the work concerned. The review is not just a means for the reviewer to exercise a prejudice which has nothing to do with the work concerned.

Such reviews are an insult to the intelligence of a reader. They are usually so obviously biased that the reviewer ends up looking very silly.

Obviously, no one is going to label his or her work in this way. It is useful, however, to have an information classification into which such works can be placed. The label can be applied by the reader or by others.

The codes are not intended to be a classification of information as such but more of a 'pre-code' to indicate what is coming next. The use of a label like 7/6 is that one person can then transmit his or her opinion to others and so provide them with the pre-code service.

CODE 7

7/7 This is advocacy or case-making. The writer of the material is seeking to make a case. The intention of the writer is to suggest a point of view and to offer support for it.

The soundness of the reasons put forward and the honesty of the exploration are not at all guaranteed by the coding. The writer may be highly selective with information and may offer a prejudiced point of view.

The important point (and the difference from code 7/6) is that the writer is clearly setting out to make a case and is not pretending to review the matter in an objective manner.

The efforts in a courtroom of both prosecution and defence teams would fall into this category. So would many of the writings of newspaper columnists.

There is nothing wrong with advocacy so long as it is clearly indicated as such. It would be hoped that the 7/7 label would be applied to the piece by the author himself. Advocacy should not be ashamed of being one-sided – and should not pretend to be objective.

It helps if the position taken is clearly indicated at the beginning of the piece.

CODE 7

7/8 *This indicates material that is of an advertising and selling nature. This may range from a genuine attempt to show true value to exaggerated puffery.*

Most people can recognize advertising copy so there is no harm in labelling it in advance.

Advertising copy is a form of advocacy. There is an attempt to show why a particular purchase would be in the best interests of the purchaser.

Once again, even if the producer of the material was unwilling to apply this label, the label remains available for others to apply.

CODE 7

7/9 This is also 'selling' information but the information is put forward in a neutral way. The idea is to make known what is available in a certain field without pushing the virtues of what is available.

A schedule of courses would fall into this category. So might a catalogue of products that are available from some source.

At the extremes there is a big difference between 7/8 and 7/9. In the middle they can get pretty close and it may be difficult to separate low-key advertising from product information.

There is also an overlap with 7/1, which simply puts forward factual information.

CODE 7

7/10 This indicates chat or conversation.

The information has value for those involved in the conversation. People may be trying to make a point and may be quoting facts. The distinguishing factor is that the information is directed at those taking part.

The tone of the conversation may range from abuse to romance. You do not have to get involved unless you want to get involved. The quality of the chat may be high or extremely low.

CODE 7

7/11 This is the fine print. These are the 'footnotes'. This label indicates further detail. There is amplification of points already made. There are further references.

Sometimes you need the fine print and sometimes you do not. Having a clear identification of the fine print makes it easier to find – and easier to avoid.

In general, the fine print is only of value if you have already shown interest in the main text. The fine print is the following up of this interest.

CODE 7

7/12 Proposals, propositions, suggestions, offerings, etc. This may include suggested contracts. Something is being put forward for consideration and possible action.

What is important with this label is the 'invitation' aspect. The receiver of the information is invited to consider the suggestion and perhaps to respond to it.

This invitation is much more specific than the invitation offered by general advertising.

Contracts are a form of invitation in which both parties are invited to work together in a defined way.

Action suggestions and alternative action suggestions also come under the 7/12 indicator.

The information here is about things which have not yet happened.

CODE 7

7/13 This indicates hate, bigotry and a strong emotional outpouring.

It may be said that such material is so obvious that there is hardly a need for an indicator.

Ordinary advocacy sets out to make a case as in 7/7. Where emotion has clearly taken over from reason the matter fits more suitably under 7/13.

Although the indicator is normally applied to negative emotions it might equally be applied to positive emotions if they were also excessive.

Note that the emphasis is on 'outpouring' rather than 'appeal'.

CODE 7

7/14 This indicates advice, help, motivation, self-help, training, etc.

The material is intended to be of value to the receiver, not because of its pure information content, but because it may change the receiver in some way: behaviour, attitudes, values, perception, etc.

The category is a wide one and may range from technical training to stuff that is very 'preachy'.

CODE 7

7/15 *This indicates 'forms to fill in'. Forms of any sort come into this category.*

Forms are requests for specific information laid out in a specific way. Forms are a request for information rather than offered information.

There is still a value in having an indicator that signals 'forms' even though these are fairly obvious once they have been seen. In searching through an index, you would not see the form itself. The indicator would lead you to the form.

In preparing information you could guide the user to the 7/15 section which would contain the forms.

YOUTH CODE
CODE 8

Awkwardness, shyness, embarrassment and inarticulacy are as much a barrier to communication as lack of concepts. It may well be possible to describe a complex situation in a fluent and competent way. But if the situation is stressful and the communicator is young, then the 'possible' fluent description is simply not available, so communication does not take place. That makes things even more stressful. Add to that the very important consideration that the other party does not seem willing to listen at all. It may be theoretically possible to make fine speeches but if the other party is not listening, the fine speeches have little communication value.

It is for all these reasons that the youth code has a direct and immediate value. To be able to sum up a complex emotional situation in a single code is useful. Unlike situations where the code is a convenience, the youth code may be a necessity.

Obviously the code works best if both sides are fully aware of it. Therefore there have to be advantages for both sides to encourage a willingness to use the code.

If only one side is willing to use the code, then the code can still be used as a supplement to other communication. In time at least some of the items on the code will be learned through repetition. There is certainly nothing to be lost by using the code. The time taken is tiny. The potential benefits are huge.

The code would normally be used from parents to children or the other way around. It could also be used in any adult-to-youth or youth-to-adult situation.

Code 8
The Youth Code

8/1 *I am in trouble and I need your help. I do not want a lecture or a judgement. I do not want you to jump down my throat – but I do need to talk to you. Is that possible?*

Parents are often seen as a source of admonition, lectures and disapproval. Too often this is necessary because the energy of youth can seem to take wrong turnings.

The difficulty is to have some way of laying aside this 'judgement' role in order to take up an 'advice and help' role. Code 8/1 is a request for just such a switch.

There may be many ways of expressing the same thing in normal language but none of them would have the clarity and directness of 8/1 as an accepted code.

Some parents manage very well the complex role of guide, judge and friend. Some find themselves, even unwillingly, emphasizing one role over the others. All roles may be required. Different temperaments, of both parent and child, seem to encourage one or other role to become dominant.

Code 8/1 provides a formal request to step into the 'friend and adviser' role.

CODE 8

The request may be ignored but at least there is now a mechanism for making the request.

Note that the emphasis in this code is on 'trouble'. The person is in 'trouble' and is asking for help. Other codes have less urgency.

CODE 8

8/2 I am having difficulty making a decision. I am having difficulty making up my mind. I would like to discuss the matter with you. Don't tell me what to do – but help me to make up my mind.

The important point here is that the code user does not want to be told what to do but wants help in making his or her decision. It may be a matter of giving advice based on a wider experience. It may be a matter of directing attention to something which is being overlooked. It may be just an independent view which is not biased by emotions.

There are many ways in which a decision can be helped. Once the broader picture can be seen the decision becomes much easier. If you have a good road map it is easier to choose the right road.

The parent or adult must resist the temptation of providing the decision. At worst the adult may say: 'If I was in your position, this is what I would probably do . . .'

It is best to say something like: 'That is the way I see the situation but the decision is yours to make.' Different values and different long-term goals can lead to different decisions based on the same input.

CODE 8

8/3 I am confused. I am in a muddle. I need clarification. I need another point of view. Perhaps you can help me. It is clarification rather than advice that I need.

When you do not have much experience of life, when emotions are involved and when relationships are sensitive, things can become very confusing. Any objective and dispassionate view can be of help. Any adult might provide such an outside view. A parent is more accessible – if that parent is willing to help.

As before, the temptation to preach and to impose a point of view must be resisted. The request is specifically a request for help 'in understanding'. This is different from help in making a decision or solving a problem.

The more the adult is willing to provide exactly the help that is needed the more that request will be used in the future. If the adult uses the opportunity for the usual preaching then the code loses its specific value.

It is no sin to understand something. It should be natural to ask for help in understanding.

CODE 8

8/4 There is something that I need to talk about. There is something that I need to discuss. I need to talk and I need you to listen.

The emphasis is directly on 'listen'. This is a very general request and could be used to cover the preceding requests, which are more focused.

Often, being able to talk to someone about something clears the mind and clarifies the issues. Even if the other person does no more than keep awake and nod from time to time, this is of high value.

The effort to talk and to express ideas and to describe a situation makes it easier to deal with that situation. Talking to yourself does not work. Talking to your peers may be difficult because the subject may be private and embarrassing. Furthermore you do not want the subject matter to become gossip.

A parent or close adult is the ideal person to talk to – if that person is willing to listen. The person 'talked to' does not have to keep totally silent. That person may ask questions, offer perceptions and suggest options.

It is important to remember that this particular request is not for help in solving a problem or for help in making a decision. The request is directly for someone to listen.

The request may indeed evolve into a request for advice, but this is the choice of the person making the request. It is not up to the listener to provide more than is directly requested.

CODE 8

8/5 I would like an honest and direct answer to the question that I am going to ask you. Please do not use the question as an opportunity to give advice or judgement. I would just like an answer to the question. Please answer the question as it is – do not change it into another question that may be easier to answer.

People are often unwilling to answer questions because an answer is a commitment. People are also wary of being led into a trap through being asked a series of linked questions. The famous Greek philosopher, Socrates, did this all the time. He would ask apparently simple questions with fairly obvious answers. The listener would be led, step by step, to an apparently logical conclusion that he would never have agreed to.

The natural response to this request might be:
    '. . . depends on the question.'
    '. . . depends on the context.'
    '. . . if I am able to answer it.'

To which might be added: 'if it is your business'. Parents are willing to help but do not have to agree to subject themselves to interrogations.

It is always possible to have a repertoire of stock answers:
    'That question cannot be answered without more specific details.'
    'The answer to that question depends on the context.'
    'It all depends on your values and on what you want to achieve.'

Being willing to answer a question is still very helpful.

CODE 8

8/6 This thing is really very important to me. You may not think so. You may not understand. It would be difficult to explain. Trust me, this thing is important to me.

8/7 This is something I really, really want to do. I hope I can have your approval and support.

There is an overlap between 8/6 and 8/7. The difference is that with 8/7 the youngster is willing to explain why he or she wants to do something.

It may be a choice, an ambition, an ultimate goal or a course of action. The person is asking for:

lack of resistance
approval
encouragement
support.

There are tennis prodigies whose parents encouraged them. There are musical geniuses whose parents pushed them. There may be a fine line between encourage and push. There is a sharp distinction between the parents' choice of direction and the youngster's choice of direction. This code signals the youngster's choice and asks for parental approval and support.

'I hope you will not disapprove of this and resist it' is a large part of the request, since parents are often perceived to be in a permanent disapproving mode (based on superior experience).

CODE 8

8/6, 8/7

If the person asked by the code cannot approve the proposed course of action then he or she must say so clearly. There is still a high value in having a simple means of making the request.

The request is not for a blank cheque; it is a 'hope'.

Young people are often difficult to understand because they may be involved in complex relationships which adults cannot perceive.

There may be reasons why something is important which would sound totally trivial and absurd to an adult. That is why the youngster does not want to spell out the reasons. At the same time the reasons are very real and important to the youngster.

The request is a request for trust. It is a request to trust the values of a younger world. To a youngster it is very important to establish and keep a position in a 'peer group'. To an adult this may not seem important at all.

To a youngster what seems to be important is indeed important. The youngster may be mistaken from an adult point of view but the youngster is living in a young world, not the adult one.

Any request for 'trust' can be abused if the request is made too often and is used to cover matters which should really be discussed. It is up to youngsters not to abuse this particular code because if it is abused it may no longer be available when it is really needed.

CODE 8

8/8 Sure, let's talk. Let's discuss things. I am willing to listen without judging. I have the time. So let's talk.

This is the positive reply to all the different requests for discussion, talking, advice, etc.

There is a commitment of time and motivation. There is a willingness to talk on a 'discussion' rather than a judgemental basis. There is a commitment to talk as 'friend to friend'. At the same time the wisdom and experience of the adult is available.

It is obvious that the code should not be abused. If the adult agrees to talk on a 'friend' basis and then switches to the judgement role, then the code loses credibility for that person. To abuse a code is to lose a code. There may be a very temporary advantage but once credibility is lost it cannot be regained.

Agreeing to 'talk' is as significant as fighters agreeing to negotiate.

CODE 8

8/9 What is troubling you? What is the matter? Tell me the problem.

Most parents are very good at recognizing when their children have a problem. Most children who have a problem know the behaviour and 'codes' which will signal to a parent that there is a problem.

This particular code is possibly redundant because parents are always saying: 'What is the matter with you?' The value of the code is that it is simple, direct, neutral and impersonal. It is a genuine inquiry as to what the matter might be.

Many youngsters find it difficult to launch into their concerns and problems unless they are specifically asked to. The code provides the request.

The code covers a broad spectrum from serious matters like a career choice to a minor upset such as when a youngster seems to have been favoured in some small matter.

CODE 8

8/10 What do you really think and feel about this? I would like an honest answer – not one designed to please me.

Many of the youth code items seem to be directed by a parent or adult to a youngster. Many of them, however, can equally be used by a youngster talking to a parent or adult. This particular code is a good example.

A youngster may ask what a parent really thinks and feels about some proposed action. In exactly the same way a parent might ask a youngster what he or she feels about something; for example going to live in another place.

The emphasis is on 'really', and on honesty. The code indicates that it is all right to be honest and blunt. There is no need for the diplomatic reply.

The answer should not require the listener to read between the lines or to interpret what has been said. The answer should be clear and honest.

'You asked for my honest feeling. This is what I feel.'

The person replying has been given full permission to be as honest as he or she can.

If you do not want an honest answer then do not use this code!

CODE 8

8/11 What are your intentions? What are you plans? What are you going to do?

The range is great:
> 'What are you going to do this afternoon?'
> 'What are you going to do this summer?'
> 'What career are you going to choose?'
> 'What are you going to do with your life?'

The framework or context needs to be made very clear if it has not already been made clear by the context of the conversation.

The request does not demand a great deal of detail. It is up to the person who responds to choose the level of detail. It is possible to reply in very broad terms:
> 'I intend to see how things go.'
> 'I have not decided yet.'
> 'I want a career helping people.'

If the questioner wants more details these can be asked for.

In a way this code 'puts someone on the spot'. There is a direct request. The questioner may already have some idea of what the answer might be, but is now asking a direct question.

It is also possible for a youngster to ask the question of an adult.

CODE 8

8/12 *You are behaving like a spoiled brat. You are being very selfish. You cannot always get your own way.*

Some youngsters would never merit this warning. Others merit it all the time.

The code makes very clear what the parent or adult thinks. The level of behaviour which might trigger this code will vary from family to family but the meaning is clear enough.

The code encapsulates all the disapproval and displeasure there may be. It saves a lot of energy in scolding or shouting.

Because the code can be used in a cold and unemotional way the impact is greater than an emotional tirade.

As with several other codes, this code should not be overused or abused. If it comes to be used on every occasion of mild disapproval then it becomes devalued and is no longer available when it is really needed.

8/13 Show some manners and respect. Don't behave in that boorish and oafish manner. Be civilized – or try to be.

This is a broad and general request for behaviour that is more civilized. Usually, crass behaviour is not deliberate but merely 'unthinking'.

'Respect' is the key word. Civilization is built on respect. If you respect other people then your behaviour will always be civilized.

The request is not so much for the niceties of manner, which can often be forgotten, but for respect for others.

A smoker is not deliberately setting out to upset other people but may have a lack of respect for their preference for a clean atmosphere.

Selfishness and lack of respect overlap but are not quite the same thing. You can be selfish and still respect others.

CODE 8

8/14 For some reason you are in a difficult and cranky mood. Could you snap out of it?

This is not a request for the reasons behind the cranky mood. It is simply a statement that 'your mood is cranky'. It is intended to make the person aware of this crankiness.

The cause may be tiredness, a hangover, the time of the month (PMT), preoccupation with a problem, etc.

The code really signals: 'Are you aware that you are being difficult and cranky?'

It is difficult to have insight into your own moods unless they are extreme. The code is a friendly reminder of how you are behaving. It is not intended to be a condemnation.

'Mum's 8/14 this morning.'
'Towards the end of a holiday everyone gets a bit 8/14.'

There is some overlap with the mood code (code 10).

CODE 8

8/15 Don't sulk. It won't get you anywhere.

This code is very simple and very direct. You are sulking. Stop sulking.

A genuine sulk is an exaggerated posture to show that someone is upset and wants others to know all about it. This 'upset' is to be used as a sort of lever to get what is wanted.

On the basis that parents may not like to see their loved ones upset, the sulk has a purpose. The more successful sulks are in achieving their objective, the more frequently they may be used. The code makes clear to everyone that 'the sulking game is being used'.

It is not always easy to distinguish between a sulk and a genuine hurt or disappointment. The outward symptoms of withdrawal and quietness may be the same. The difference is that one is a reaction which cannot be helped (hurt) and the other is a deliberate act with a purpose (sulk).

People who have developed the fine art of sulking may really find it difficult to get out of the habit. The code may help by increasing insight and by suggesting it is silly.

CODE 8

8/16 Clean up the mess. Tidy up. Put things away.

Since younger people have a different sense of order from older people this may well become the most used of all the codes.

If you know exactly where everything is, why is it a disorder? There is some truth in that claim. Adults believe, however, that a training in tidiness carries over into many other things – including thinking. Also, if anyone else has to deal with the situation then a 'personal order' may well be total disorder to anyone else.

For whatever reason, justified or not, parents are forever exhorting their children to be more tidy.

'Let's have a bit of 8/16 here.'

'8/16 please.'

'You can – but after an 8/16.'

It is possible to extend this code from its immediate meaning to different situations.

'8/16 your thinking on this.'

'This is a financial mess; 8/16 is going to be the mode for the next few months.'

'He's not very 8/16, is he?'

CODE 8

8/17 Be nice to your brothers and sisters.

The number and genders do not matter. Be nice to your sibling or siblings.

Petty meanness and squabbles are part of family life. One or other or both parties are to blame. This code is a general request to stop it, cool it, lay off, take time out, etc.

'Whoever is to blame, stop it!'

Quite apart from tense moments the code is a general exhortation to be nice to other siblings. It may be that a boy or girl needs help. It may be that a boy or girl is being left out. There are many situations which might benefit from increased 'niceness'.

Long-standing sibling jealousy and rivalry are not likely to be affected by this code and need deeper attention. The code can, however, deal with moment-to-moment troubles.

CODE 8

8/18 It would be nice if you could help. It would be nice if you could contribute.

There are times when some members of a family are busy and others seem to be lazing about. This is very much an individual choice within every family. Some families have clearly defined 'work roles' and each person carries out his or her own function. Other families like everyone to share chores all the time. In addition there are special situations, like preparing for a party, where everyone is needed.

The code is a gentle invitation to get involved and to contribute. It is not meant to be a fierce command or a condemnation of apparent laziness. It is more a 'suggestion' than an order.

People do not like to interfere because this can suggest that the person doing something is incapable or incompetent. Also, some people do not like help and feel they can manage better and faster on their own. So having a code which signals clearly that some help would be appreciated has a high value.

The code is also of value between youngsters or even between adults.

There is a fine distinction between 'It would be nice if you could help' and 'You should be contributing.' The code covers both meanings.

CODE 8

8/19 Let's have some peace and quiet. Stop that racket or go somewhere else.

Youth is energetic and exuberant. Age sometimes relishes tranquillity. The interface between the two is not always easy.

'Peace and quiet' is a value. It is perfectly legitimate to request it. You may have a right to make a noise but you do not have a right to impose the noise on others (as with smoking). So it is a matter of quietening down or going somewhere else – if that is possible.

There may be households which insist on quietness all the time. That may be rather restricting if there is no place to go to make a noise.

The code is a request, from time to time, for peace and quiet. Overuse of the code diminishes its value.

'Some 8/19 please.' The strangeness and directness of the code may be more compelling than just asking for quiet.

CODE 8

8/20 *Don't be unreasonable.*

This is a powerful and direct request. It may be used by an adult to a youngster but may also be used the other way around.

'Being unreasonable' may mean being emotional. An emotional position has been taken and is only sustained by emotion. The code could equally have indicated: 'Don't be so emotional.'

'Being unreasonable' might also mean just producing a decision, request or order without showing any reasoned support.

'Being unreasonable' might also mean producing some very poor reasons for doing something. Or not following a logical chain of reason.

The code is a request to explain, to be logical and to be reasonable.

There are times when it is simply not possible to give reasons. A decision may be based on great experience or on intuition which cannot be itemized.

No one is obliged to provide reasons just because they have been requested. The code simply indicates that something appears to be 'unreasonable'.

The main use of the code may well be to switch from the emotion mode to the reason mode.

CODE 8

8/21 I need attention. Don't ignore me.

This is a very valuable code because it is almost impossible for a youngster to ask for attention directly. You can seek attention through behaviour or being difficult, etc., but to ask directly for attention is extremely difficult.

There are times when people need attention. There are times when people feel they are being neglected. Often this is in fact the case. Quiet people often get neglected because everyone else thinks they are perfectly capable of getting on by themselves.

To ask for attention seems weak and feeble. It should not be and it need not be. So having a code that signals this request is useful.

There are people who demand attention all the time. There are dependent people who cannot cope on their own. The code is not designed to help this behaviour. The code is for occasional use by those who really need it.

It may be that a decision is being made and someone is being left out of the discussion. The code signals: 'I am here and I am involved. I want to be considered.'

CODE 8

8/22 Thank you. Thank you very much. I appreciate what you are doing or have done. I want you to know that I am very grateful.

This may be the most important code of all. Saying thank-you is never full enough. No matter how grateful a person may be it is difficult to say thank-you with enough intensity. So the code provides a powerful way of indicating appreciation and gratitude.

The existence of this code does not exclude other expressions of gratitude. The code can simply be added to these.

Many codes are requests or demands or even expressions of disapproval. Code 8/22 is the opposite. It expresses gratitude.

CODE 8

8/23 *That is fine. That is just right. That is perfect. I like that very much. Also, congratulations, you have done very well. That is excellent.*

This code expresses satisfaction. You like the idea. You like the plan. You like the meal. Code 8/23 is the seal of approval.

This is not specifically restricted to youth situations. It could be used anywhere. There is, however, a need for it in the youth code because there is a need to express approval and satisfaction.

A job well done needs appreciation.

There is a difference between 8/22 and 8/23. If someone has done something for you then appreciation and gratitude are in order. If someone has done something that is good but has nothing to do with you then appreciation and approval are in order.

So the code signals 'approval' by the person sending the code.
　'I approve of this suggestion.'
　'I approve of your winning the junior tennis tournament.'

MEETINGS
CODE 9

I once suggested that meetings should be held with all the chairs at the table, facing outwards. This way everyone could listen to everyone else but not see their faces or body language.

The reason behind this suggestion is that body language, deliberately or otherwise, very often signals negativity or disagreement.

When people are sitting passively in a meeting listening to one person talking should they be able to communicate their thoughts and feelings?

The meeting code put forward here is a concrete means of allowing listeners to communicate with the speaker. The listeners can use the code to communicate directly without saying a word.

This meetings code is not intended to be used throughout a meeting at every conversational point. If, however, a presentation is being made, then the listeners can communicate via the code.

The code would not be spoken but would be written, in large numbers, on tent-shaped cards which a participant would have before him or her. A blank card could be displayed or any one of the code numbers.

Although this code is intended for meetings it could also be applied to lectures – or even in school. Not all the codes would be applicable but a few of them would make sense.

If something has not been expressed clearly, should you not be able to indicate this? If you are not clear what the conclusion is, should you not

CODE 9

be able to ask for this? These are the sort of communications which the code makes possible.

The speaker may choose to ignore the code or may seek to respond to it. Different participants may have different needs and it may not be possible to respond to all these needs.

This code can be overused and abused, as with many other codes. If the speaker feels this is the case, then he or she can ignore the code. When everyone seems to be offering the same code, however, the speaker would do well to respond to it.

This code offers a communication that is simply not available at the moment other than through facial expression and body language.

Code 9
Meetings

9/1 *I am confused. I am lost. I cannot follow you. Please repeat. Please clarify. Please simplify. I do not follow your line of thought. I do not understand what you are saying. This is too complicated. You are not communicating with me.*

This is a powerful code. If a listener does not understand or follow what is being communicated, communication is not taking place. Everyone has a right to indicate that he or she is not following what is being said.

It may be that a particular person has a hangover or is slow-witted, but that would be an unfair assumption. If more than one person shows code 9/1 then something needs to be done. Even if it is only one person, the speaker should make an effort to repeat and simplify what has been said.

There are subjects which are indeed complex. But if you are communicating such subjects you have an obligation to make them understandable to your audience. It may be very difficult but that is the speaker's problem. The speaker cannot shift the problem to the audience and tell them to be smarter.

CODE 9

9/1

If the listeners are being asked to consider, react to or decide upon what is being said, then they have to understand what is being said.

Unless the code is being abused (by someone who understands perfectly well), then the speaker should seek to take it into account.

With code 9 there is no longer any need for someone to sit there in confused darkness at a presentation.

CODE 9

9/2 Do not assume that we know the current situation. Please spell it out. What is the background? What is happening? What is currently being proposed? Give the overall perspective. Spell out the situation even if you think we know it. Put me in the picture.

Some people in the room may be much more familiar with the current situation than others. The speaker may assume that everyone knows the current situation and that he or she would be wasting their time going over it again. This may be so, but code 9/2 allows participants to signal that they are not fully in the picture.

All suggested changes need to be judged against the present position, so a very clear understanding of the present position is essential.

It may be that those present 'should' know the present position. That is irrelevant. They may need to be reminded of it. Many people serve on several different boards and cannot be expected to remember the nuances of the situation in each organization.

How much detail the speaker chooses to give in setting out the present position is up to the speaker and his or her assessment of the needs of the audience. The person who needs to be 'put in the picture' may signal that he or she is not yet in the picture – or may simply ask questions.

As with code 9/1, if only one person signals 9/2 then the matter need not be attended to in detail. But if more people choose the same signal more effort is evidently needed.

165

CODE 9

9/3 *Get to the point. What do you propose? What do you want to see happen? What is the concrete suggestion? Exactly what do you want to happen?*

Occasionally, presentations are a report on what has happened. They may also be an exploration of a field with no further intention than understanding of the current situation. More often, presentations have some proposal to put forward. Some change is suggested. Perhaps there is a decision to be made and the presentation backs one side or the other.

Code 9/3 asks the speaker to come to the point. What is the purpose behind the presentation?

Some presentations may state the purpose up front. Others have so much preamble that listeners have no idea what is happening.

'Cut the crap and get to the point' is what code 9/3 is all about.

CODE 9

9/4 Could you summarize what you have been saying? Could you repeat the main points? Could you please bring your talk to an end?

Code 9/4 is a very polite way of suggesting that the speaker come to the end of his or her presentation. There is a direct request for a summary. There is a request to have the main points repeated.

If the speaker has not yet covered an important area then the speaker should signal this and move at once to this area. At the same time the speaker needs to be conscious that he or she has been asked to hurry up.

A summary is broader than a conclusion. The summary will also include the points that led to the conclusion. From the summary it may be possible for listeners to reach a conclusion different from that suggested by the speaker.

CODE 9

9/5 *More information is needed at this point. I need more information. Can we have some facts and figures? Where is the hard data? Is there any data to support the view?*

A philosophical discussion can operate in broad generalities without ever touching reality. Code 9/5 is a specific request for data.

Because of the way the code cards will be used it may be difficult to request data at one specific point. The card may not be shown at this point or, if shown, may not be noticed. So code 9/5 is a general request for underlying data (if there is any).

If there is no information, then the speaker is being asked to state this. At once the presentation is seen as speculation and philosophy.

The request is really a request for a 'reality check'. In many cases the data will have been presented in written form to the participants beforehand. The data may also be shown as slides or computer-generated displays.

Sometimes there is too much information and not enough use of the information. The code applies to situations where there seems to be a need for some hard data.

CODE 9

9/6 What are the benefits? Why is this worth doing? Why is this a good idea? Why is this going to work? Why does this make sense? What are the advantages?

Code 9/6 is a direct request to have the benefits spelled out clearly. The benefits may indeed be implicit in what has been said, but they do need to be laid out.

This code is not a request for a full scan but for a focus on benefits. How strong are the benefits? Who will benefit? On what do the benefits depend? How vulnerable are the benefits to change? Under what conditions are the benefits obtained?

Without benefits, no idea or proposal is a good one. So any proposal or change or action depends on there being considerable benefits. So what are these benefits?

CODE 9

9/7 *What is the downside? What are the risks? What are the drawbacks? What might go wrong? What is weak about the idea? What is dangerous about the idea? Could the idea go bad?*

Code 9/7 is obviously the counterpart to code 9/6. This is a specific request for the spelling out of risks and dangers.

In practice there are probably three sorts of risks.

There is the risk that the idea will simply not work at all. It may also work poorly.

There is the risk that the idea might work but will not deliver the benefits that have been promised and hoped for. These anticipated benefits do not appear.

There is the risk of actual danger, damage or downside from the implementation of the idea. For example, a competitor might be stirred to hit back very hard.

Even though it is intended for meetings, code 9/7 could also have a general use.

CODE 9

9/8 *This is a weak case. I am doubtful. I am not convinced. I do not agree with the argument. I do not agree with the conclusion. I am not on your side.*

This code signals a general disagreement. The difficulty of using the code to disagree over one particular point is that the code needs to be attached to just that point. It may be possible to flash the code 9/8 card and then to state the disagreement. It would be tedious if this were to be done too often.

The code simply indicates that the presenter has not convinced the participant. The case may still be a good one but the presenter has not made the case out adequately. In practice, it may be difficult (and even unnecessary) to decide whether the fault is that of the presenter or of the proposal itself.

The simplest statement of code 9/8 is: 'I am not convinced.'

9/9 I fully agree. I am convinced. I have followed your line of reasoning and I agree with you. You have made out a strong case. You can count on my support. I am on your side.

This is the opposite of code 9/8. The participant is signalling agreement. The case has been made well.

Now it may be that the participant started the meeting in favour of the proposal. Or the participant may have been neutral and is now convinced. It may even be that the participant started out against the idea and has changed his or her mind.

The use of this code is a form of visible voting. It is an encouragement to the speaker. It could also be seen as a signal that the speaker does not need to go on.

While disapproval is quite easily signalled by facial expression and body language, approval is more difficult to signal. In any case, signalling with facial expression or body language is only for the moment; displayed code cards can stay there for a long time.

CODE 9

9/10 This stuff is irrelevant. This stuff has nothing to do with the main point or the purpose of the meeting. This is a deviation. This is a distraction. Can we please get back to the purpose of the meeting? No matter how interesting this stuff might be, it does not really help.

This code would be frequently used if people had the courage.

Faced with this code the speaker needs to show why the material is in fact relevant to the meeting. There might be a high relevance which is not obvious. If so, the speaker needs to make it obvious.

Although this code is intended to be used in a presentation, it could equally well be used during the general conversation of a meeting to indicate that the whole meeting had gone off track.

If one person uses code 9/10 it is significant; if many participants come to show code 9/10 on their cards it becomes serious.

MOOD CODE
CODE 10

I am told that there is a corporation where every morning each executive switches on a coloured light bulb beside his name at the entrance. A green bulb means: 'I have time. My door is open. I am available. I am willing to listen.' A red bulb means: 'I am under pressure. I am very busy. Don't hassle me. Don't bother me unless it is extremely urgent.'

How do people signal their moods?

If you look grumpy, is it because someone has upset you? Is it because you have a hangover or are not feeling well? Is it because you are worried about some problem? Is it because you are tired or under pressure? Is it because you are depressed?

People have to pick up mood clues from facial expression, tone of voice, behaviour and general crankiness. This is a very clumsy and crude method – even for those who are very good at picking up the clues.

Very few people find it easy to indicate their mood to others. The most people manage is 'I am tired' or 'I am under pressure'. To this might be added: 'I got to bed late last night' (meaning 'I have a hangover').

Would it not be convenient if our mood was written boldly on our foreheads so that everyone could tell at once what mood we were in? They could then adjust their behaviour accordingly.

When I have suggested to children the wearing of a mood badge which they could adjust to show their mood of the moment, they have not liked the idea. They fear that adults will take advantage of this openness.

CODE 10

The purpose of a 'mood code' is to provide individuals with a way of being able to signal their mood, and so facilitate dealings with others. If your secretary knows you are in a 'difficult' mood, then she knows how to deal with you.

The mood code is not an imposition but a benefit.

The main use of the mood code may be in the business world but the code could be used domestically or in any other environment.

Code 10
Mood Code

10/1 Would you like to tell me what your mood is today? What is your mood right now? Perhaps you would like to indicate what your mood is? What's up?

Code 10/1 is meant to be a respectful inquiry. It is not a demand to know someone else's mood.

'Would you like the opportunity to tell me your mood – using the mood code?'

There may be no response. There does not have to be a response. The person asked should see the benefit of defining his or her mood in a more definite way than through behaviour. 'I can tell you my mood. You do not have to guess at it or try to figure it out from my behaviour.'

Just as you might say, 'A penny for your thoughts', you might casually say, '10/1 to you.'

CODE 10

10/2 I am happy. I am in a happy mood. Things are going well. The mood is positive and good.

Code 10/2 is a very general upbeat response. More detailed definitions of a good mood are given later in the code.

Note that code 10/2 is more than neutral. It is more than 'business as usual'. There is a definite 'happy' component.

The provision of codes 10/2, 10/3 and 10/4 is to allow a broad, general response to be given. If you wish you can just remember these three codes.

The use of 10/2 should at least be sincere. It should not just be the easiest way to respond to the question: 'What is your mood?'

CODE 10

10/3 *The mood is neutral and normal. It is not specially happy nor is it specially unhappy. It is business as usual. It is the baseline mood. My usual mood.*

Of course, the 'baseline' will vary with the speaker. Some people's baseline is normally cheerful. For other people the baseline may be more sombre.

Code 10/3 signals normality. There is nothing specially upbeat nor anything downbeat.

It is very likely that in such situations code 10/1 would not have been used in the first place. If the mood seems normal enough, there is really no need to ask what the mood might be.

'Neutral' does not imply empty, colourless or apathetic. Neutral simply means 'usual' or 'normal' for that person.

'It's a 10/3 day.'
'Just the usual, 10/3.'
'What makes you think it is not the usual 10/3?'

CODE 10

10/4 *This is the broad, generic 'unhappy' response. It is downbeat. I am unhappy. I am not happy. I am not feeling good. I am below my baseline mood.*

Code 10/4 is a broad and simple signal. The signal suggests that all is not well.

There is no indication why things are not well. This could be asked in direct question: 'What is the matter?'

There are other codes which are much more specific as to why things are not right. These could be used directly without ever using 10/4.

There is, however, a value in having 10/4 as a generic response. It may be easier to remember than all the other codes.

There might be some point in using a double code. For example, someone might say: 'Code 10/4 and code 10/5.' This means: 'I am not happy because I am too busy and overworked.' There is not much advantage, however, in doing this rather than just using 10/5 on its own. There may be the value of emphasis.

Where the nature of the 'not well' mood cannot be defined by any of the other codes, then the general nature of 10/4 becomes an advantage.

CODE 10

10/5 I am overworked. I am very busy. There is far too much to do. I am being stretched.

Note that there is no suggestion in code 10/5 that the person is stressed or cannot cope with the excessive workload. The code is a simple statement that there is a lot to do. The person using the code is not even complaining. The person is simply indicating that his or her mood is related to the great amount of work that needs to be done.

It may be that at certain times of the year there is a larger amount of work than usual. It may be that some special project requires extra work.

In all cases, code 10/5 is not designed as a comment on organizational efficiency. It is simply a statement of mood related to the large amount of work to be done.

The advantage of such a code is that it clearly indicates that the 'unhappiness' is not due to some other cause, such as displeasure with an individual.

CODE 10

10/6 *I am under pressure. I am being hassled. There are many demands to be met. People are getting at me.*

Code 10/6 is rather different from an excessive workload. The key word is 'pressure'. The person is responding that he or she is being 'pressured' over some matter.

Pressure may arise from multiple demands. Pressure may arise from unrealistic demands. Pressure may arise from exaggerated expectations. Pressure may even arise because the person is not used to pressure. Whatever the cause of the pressure (whether it is reasonable or not), code 10/6 indicates a mood related to being pressured.

It must be quite clear that a person who has indicated 10/6 should not be subjected to yet more pressure!

10/7 *I am tense. For some reason I feel tension. It may be a combination of factors. Whatever the reason, I feel tense today.*

Tense is the opposite of relaxed. There may be a specific cause of the tension. More usually, several things may have come together to give this feeling of tension.

People who are tense tend to be snappy, irritable and quick-tempered. Code 10/7 indicates that this bad temper is due to underlying tension and not to what is happening at the moment.

At the same time code 10/7 is an appeal for relaxation: sport, humour, music, massage, etc.

Sometimes tension may be a reaction to something specific like a disagreeable meeting that has just taken place.

CODE 10

10/8 *I am just very tired. I have been doing a lot lately. Or, I have just got back from a long trip. Or, I did not get to bed until late last night. There may be various causes why I am feeling so tired. But I am tired.*

Code 10/8 indicates that the mood arises from nothing more than simple 'tiredness'. Tiredness is a natural reaction of the body to demands made upon it. Tiredness is no one's fault.

The main point about code 10/8 is that it explains a mood on the basis that is no one's fault. It is true that the code may be misused as a general explanation of bad temper and irritability. Should this occur then the people around will start to give a different meaning to the code.

'Yes, I am in a difficult mood. But it is no one's fault. I am simply very tired.'

The signal is also a request to be allowed to have a rest.

CODE 10

10/9 *I am depressed. I am going through a phase of depression. This is no one's fault. It happens to many people from time to time.*

Depression is as much a clinical fact as influenza, arthritis or a peptic ulcer. In most cases the depression is very mild and soon passes. In a few cases there may be a need for treatment. What is known as 'bipolar illness' or 'manic depression' refers to the more severe variety. A large number of people suffer from mild depression.

Now it may be that no one will want to acknowledge depression because it may be seen as a sort of stigma and a barrier to promotion. At the same time it is useful to have a code which allows someone to acknowledge depression in a straightforward manner.

This particular code may even be more useful in domestic and non-business situations than in business.

Once again, the code signals that the mood is real but that it is not the fault of anyone.

CODE 10

10/10 *I am unwell. I am not feeling well. I think I may be ill. I seem to have picked up a bug.*

Ill health, like tiredness, is no one's fault. Ill health may lead to a mood change that might otherwise be misinterpreted.

When someone is in a bad mood those around are quick to ascribe it to illness. Code 10/10 signals this directly. There is no longer any need to speculate as to why someone is in a difficult mood.

Once the condition has been signalled, those around will want to show some consideration in their behaviour (tea and sympathy).

This code may be abused when a person comes to use it as an 'excuse' for general bad temper. In the end this does not matter very much. If someone wants to state a false reason for the bad temper, it destroys the whole purpose of being bad-tempered (to bully, etc.).

CODE 10

10/11 I am worried about something. I am anxious about something. My mood is affected by anxiety.

The person using code 10/11 may choose to specify the cause of the anxiety.

'10/11 related to this new product launch.'

'10/11 over this sexual harassment case.'

'10/11 with regard to the inquiry.'

'10/11 about the competitor's response to our sales push.'

Anxiety is a natural state of mind provided it is not exaggerated, sustained or too frequent.

Any person, no matter how experienced, feels some anxiety about going on stage. Without this anxiety the performance can be dead.

CODE 10

10/12 I am preoccupied. I am thinking about something. There is something I have to think through. There is something I have to focus upon. My attention is tied up.

Someone who is preoccupied may have little time for the people around and may appear to be bad-tempered and irritable when this is not the case at all.

Trying to focus on some difficult matter can make someone very impatient with distractions. People may seem to be ignored and dismissed, but only because they interfere with the thinking process.

So code 10/12 has a high value in giving the correct interpretation of apparent bad behaviour.

If a person has signalled code 10/12, it is also a request to be undisturbed and to be left in peace (to do the thinking).

CODE 10

10/13 *I am in the best of moods. I am at the top of my form. I am full of energy. I want to get on with things. I am gung-ho for action. I am feeling very good indeed.*

Code 10/13 signals a positive and constructive mood. It also signals energy and the willingness to 'get on with things'. This is one of the most positive of the mood codes.

Negative moods can sometimes be picked up from facial expressions and behaviour. This is not so easy with positive moods unless they are exuberant and exaggerated. Code 10/13 signals in an unequivocal manner a mood that is well above the baseline. It is also above the more general code 10/2 (happy).

With a mood as positive as 10/13 a person may not want to wait to be asked what his or her mood might be. So the person may wish to 'announce' this mood, without being asked:
　'Today I am 10/13.'
　'I feel 10/13 today.'

There could even be a card which a person could put on his or her desk to announce to the world at large this 10/13 mood.

Code 10/13 signals a positive and constructive mood. It is not a manic mood or pure euphoria. It is a practical mood.

CODE 10

10/14 *I am annoyed and upset about a particular individual or action. I am not at all pleased about this. I hope it can be put right – or an apology offered.*

This could be called 'sulking', but no one would use this code if it were so called.

The specific subject of the annoyance should be spelled out:
    'I am 10/14 over the sloppy way you prepared that meeting.'
    '10/14 with regard to the way you contradicted me at the meeting. You should have told me before.'

CODE 10

10/15 I am upset and not pleased in a general sense. I am not happy with the way things are going. There is no one person or event about which I am unhappy. It is a general response to what I see happening.

There is a sharp contrast with 10/14, which is always focused on something in particular. Code 10/15 is more like 10/2, a general unhappiness.

You could be unhappy with the way an architect has designed the windows in a building – or you could be unhappy with the whole building. Code 10/15 is the broader type of unhappiness.

As with some of the other mood codes, the person in the 10/15 mood may want to broadcast this instead of waiting to be asked. The point about being unhappy in this broad sense is that other people should know about the unhappiness. So it is a sort of 'cosmic sulking'.

Some people use this sort of unhappiness as a way of motivating those around them who scurry about to make the boss happy.

CODE 10

10/16 *I am furious. I am very angry. And I want everyone to know that I am very angry indeed.*

This may be the strongest emotion expressed in the whole mood code. Code 10/16 is very much stronger than code 10/14, which is a sort of sulk. Code 10/16 is a rage, even though things are not thrown about.

Some people are good at the histrionics of rage: shouting, glaring, throwing things, stamping, etc. Other people may feel just as angry but do not have such a repertoire of activities. Code 10/16 allows this quieter sort of person to indicate 'rage'.

Rage is not a sustainable mood, so it is important to point out the cause of the rage before the mood passes. You can wait to be asked or you can define the cause:

'10/16 over the way they cheated on that contract.'
'10/16 over these escalating expenses.'

CODE 10

10/17 *I am becoming increasingly unhappy about the way this project is going. I am becoming more and more dissatisfied. Things are getting worse and worse.*

A very important part of code 10/17 is the 'increasing' unhappiness. Things are perceived to be getting worse. There is an escalation.

There is an element of projecting into the future and seeing things get worse. It is not just a hindsight judgement.
'10/17 about your poor performance.'
'10/17 about this court case.'
'10/17 about our ability to collect outstanding debts.'

Code 10/17 is usually applied to some specific situation, project, sector, etc. It may also be used in a general way with reference to the political or economic climate.

CODE 10

10/18 *I am disappointed. I expected better. This was not up to the usual standards. This is good, but not good enough.*

This code indicates displeasure not so much with the person as with the performance. There is the suggestion that the person is talented and could have done much better.

This is an assessment code. It is a strategy very frequently used in domestic disputes because it simultaneously praises the person's ability and condemns the expression of that ability in action.

A parent who expresses disappointment with a child's performance in an examination implies that the youngster 'could have done better' if he or she had tried harder.

CODE 10

10/19 I am stressed out at the moment. There are a lot of things going on. It is a stressful time.

Being stressed is not the same as being tired or being overworked or being anxious. It is close to being pressured or hassled except that stress need not be produced by people's demands. Bereavement can cause stress. Moving house can cause stress. Difficulty with staff can cause stress. Dealing with any difficult situation can cause stress.

In theory you can reduce stress by refusing to deal with stressful situations. But when you are hassled and pressured you cannot escape.

Like many of the mood codes, 10/19 is a plea for understanding:
'I know I am being difficult but this is because I have a lot of stress at this moment. Bear with me.'

Having moods is not so much a sign of weakness as a sign of being alive. Signalling your mood prevents misinterpretation of your behaviour.

CODE 10

10/20 I congratulate you. I applaud your success. What you have done is wonderful. I want you to know that it is really appreciated. I wish to compliment you (and the team).

This is more than just feeling pleased. There is the effort to show appreciation. There is the effort to make other people feel proud of their achievement.

Expressing appreciation is often difficult because anything that is said always seems to be inadequate. Emotional and outgoing people may manage it better. For other people flowery language and behaviour seems insincere and excessive. Code 10/20 provides a clear means of signalling appreciation.

Some people are better at delivering compliments than others. Some people are better at receiving compliments than others. Code 10/20 could be used to deliver a compliment and code 10/21 to receive a compliment.

CODE 10

10/21 Thank you. Thank you very much. I appreciate what you have done for me. I want you to know that I am grateful.

Code 10/21 is specifically directed towards someone who has done something for you. Code 10/20 congratulates someone on a performance which may not benefit you in any way.

Code 10/21 is an acknowledgement of helpful and considerate behaviour. There is a very personal element in this code. It is not just a general feeling of being pleased and happy. It is a specific appreciation of some kindness. This kindness may have been outside the line of duty but may also have been within the line of duty. A patient may thank a surgeon for performing an operation even though this is his or her job.

It might be said that thanking someone is not exactly a 'mood'. It is, nevertheless, an expression of feeling. It is a short mood.

CODE 10

10/22 *I feel frustrated. I feel thwarted. I feel blocked. I feel as if I were dancing in treacle. Or, I feel restricted. I feel I am suffocating.*

The motivation is there. The energy is there. The direction is there. But no progress can be made because something is blocking all progress.

This is a special sort of feeling because it is exasperating. All the right components of action are in place – but the action cannot proceed.

Where no action is planned a person may still feel restricted or constrained. A person may feel unable to exercise his or her skills and talents because circumstances do not allow this.

The feeling is one of being tied up or chained up. There is no freedom of action – or even of thinking. A train running on its tracks does not have the freedom of a car on the open road.

CODE 10

10/23 *I am feeling full of energy. I feel able to do anything. I am raring to go. I want to do things.*

You can be pleased about things but not very proactive. You can be happy but not very energetic. Code 10/23 signals a great amount of energy. It is true that you are unlikely to have much energy if you do not feel good. But the emphasis is on the energy.

If it is clear that someone is in mood 10/23, then that is the time to suggest changes and new projects. Just as plants require the right climate in which to grow, so projects require the right mood in which to thrive.

It is to be hoped that people in this somewhat rare mood would be able to signal this to those around them, for example by using the mood code.

As with some of the other mood codes you could have a card on your desk which signalled 10/23 to the world.

CODE 10

10/24 I am in a creative mood. I feel creative. I feel inspired. I am full of creative energy. Let's get going.

Feeling creative is a wonderful feeling. Sometimes it is enough to 'feel' creative and real creativity will follow. At other times the feeling is only the starting point and you have to work at being creative – perhaps using the tried and tested tools of lateral thinking.

The feeling of wanting to be creative is the important first step. Without such a feeling it is difficult to get going at all.

Most of the time we are content to chug along following the set patterns of behaviour because these are pretty useful. The creative feeling means a willingness to challenge the routine patterns and assumptions and to seek out new ones.

Confidence is a very important part of creativity. Truly creative people have confidence in their creativity. They have the confidence that if they set their minds to be creative about something, then they will come up with creative ideas.

In all cases the 'feeling' of being creative is a valuable mood. It is a mood that should be encouraged and should also be signalled to those around. The mood code provides a means for just such signalling: 'It's 10/24 time. Let's get going!'

DISTANCE CODE
CODE 11

This is a fun code. This is a people code. This is a hand code. This is a 'distance' code because it can be signalled over a distance.

Each of the code items has a specific hand signal. This means that you can signal to another person across a room or over a longer distance. It is enough that the other person can see you reasonably well. That is the whole purpose of the distance code.

You can use the distance code to communicate with someone you know. More often, you would use the code to get to know someone you do not yet know.

We are so used to verbal communication that we forget about visual communication. Such communication can work over distances and in noisy environments.

With many animals and birds there are visual displays which communicate some message – to another individual or to the world at large. Code 11 is directed at individuals.

Unlike most of the other codes, there is a 'question' aspect but also a 'reply' aspect.

The code can only be used by those who know the code. If you know the code but do not want to respond, then you behave as if you did not know the code.

CODE 11

The hand signals must be clear and unambiguous. The palm of the hand must be turned to face the person who is being addressed.

The code may be seen as a 'get-to-know-you' code.

Code 11
Distance Code

11/1 Do you know how to use this code? Do you use this code? Do you want to use this code right now? Let's use code 11.

If the person does not know how to use the code, it is better to know this right away. Otherwise the signals you send will be ignored or even misinterpreted.

It may be that the other party knows the code but does not want to respond to your invitation to use the code. In this case the other party could simply not respond or could use the 'no' code that is described later.

The hand signal for code 11/1 is to hold up the index finger. The palm of the hand is facing the other person and the fingers are folded down leaving the index finger upright. This finger can be seen as suggesting the figure 1.

If the other party recognizes the signal and wishes to respond in a positive way, then that party replies with an identical signal (the upright index finger). This signals both a knowledge of the code and the willingness to use it.

This simple exchange of symbols is equivalent to 'logging on'.

CODE 11

11/2 I like the look of you and I would like to meet you. Is this a good idea? What do you feel? Do you agree? Do you want to meet?

A 'get-to-know-you' meeting is being suggested. The answer may be:
1. No, I am not interested.
2. Yes.
3. Yes, but not now.

The hand signal is given by holding two fingers (index and second finger) upright with the other fingers folded down. The palm of the hand must be facing the person being signalled to. The fingers may be slightly spread to distinguish this signal from the single finger one. The two fingers symbolize two people getting together.

The person receiving this signal can ignore it and not respond at all. The person may signal 'no', using code 11/5. The person may also use code 11/4 for 'yes, but later'.

The receiver who agrees, in principle, simply repeats exactly the same signal back to the sender.

CODE 11

11/3 Fine. Let's meet. Let's meet halfway. You walk towards me and I'll walk towards you. Or, we'll meet outside. Right now.

This is the action stage. The desire to meet has been established. Now it is a matter of doing something about it.

The two suggested mechanisms of action are: meeting halfway across the room or meeting outside. The mechanisms have to be simple since they cannot be described in detail. Both parties should be able to tell from the behaviour of the other party whether the meeting is to take place outside or halfway across the room.

The emphasis is on 'right now'. If there is to be a delay then code 11/4 is signalled.

If the receiver of the message agrees, then exactly the same sign is given back. If the answer is negative, then the 'no' code (code 11/5) may be used or the signal merely ignored.

The signal is three fingers upright and the other fingers folded into the hand. The fingers can be slightly separated. The three fingers symbolize two people meeting halfway – the third finger between the other two.

Any other practical method for meeting might be used provided it can be indicated to the other party.

CODE 11

11/4 Yes, we can meet. I do want to meet. But not right now. Later. I shall signal to you when this is possible.

The signal is one of delay. The meeting has been accepted. For reasons which may not be obvious to the other party, the meeting cannot take place right now.

The signal is four fingers held up. The palm of the hand is towards the other party and the thumb is folded away. The four fingers symbolize delay because the two end fingers are 'separated' – the coming together is delayed.

The person who signals the delay now signals again when the meeting is possible. This is done by using code 11/3 (three fingers). The other party signals agreement by repeating the sign back.

The meeting sequence is code 11/1 – 2 – 3, unless a delay is introduced.

CODE 11

11/5 *The answer is 'no'. I am not interested. Don't pester me. Keep away.*

The signal is given by displaying all fingers and thumb towards the other party. The fingers are separated. It is almost as if the person is 'pushing' the other person away.

This 'no' sign is strong and probably would only be used if the other person was being a persistent nuisance. The simplest form of refusal is to ignore the signals and not to respond to them in any way.

Code 11/5 is a very clear signal showing lack of interest. It would be difficult to misinterpret this signal.

RELATIONSHIP CODES
CODE 12, 13 AND 14

There are three parts to the relationship codes.

The first part, relationship start, refers to the development and growth of a relationship. These are the opening phases and moves. Matters are moving fast – or slowly. Both parties are eager but also watchful.

The second code is relationship continue. This is the ongoing relationship. It may have been ongoing for a long time.

The third code is relationship ending. This deals with the ending of a relationship. The relationship seems to be ending. It may be possible to rescue and revive it.

The relationships are essentially the relationships between people. To some extent they can also apply to relationships between corporations in business. For this purpose just choose the codes that apply most suitably.

Each party may have a different view of the status of a relationship. The codes enable them to express this different perception.

All the situations expressed in the codes could equally be expressed in words. Sometimes such words might seem rather blunt. The neutrality of the codes allows for a more precise expression of view.

Words can be used as well as the codes:
'It seems to me that we are getting close to code —.'
'Would you agree that code — would be the most applicable?'
'Are we really in code —?'

207

CODE 12, 13 AND 14

It is possible that the situation is best described by more than one code.
    'We seem to be somewhere between code — and code —.'
    'There is a bit of code — and a bit of code — and even a bit of code —.'
    'Matters keep oscillating between code — and code —.'

In all events the codes can provide a starting point for discussions and insights into a relationship.

Code 12
Relationships Start

12/1 I am looking forward to the development of this relationship. I like you and what I know about you. I believe you also wish the relationship to develop.

The parties have met and seem to have expressed mutual interest. The stage is set for the development of a relationship.

The code is really a signal which underlines and makes visible what may already be obvious to both parties. It provides a means for affirming the developing situation. There is a formal acceptance of the situation.

Either party may still back off at this stage.

CODE 12

12/2 I have no hidden agenda or dark intentions. I like you and want to know you better. I want the relationship to develop to its appropriate level whether that is friendship or anything else.

This is an acceptance of whatever may develop. There is the basis of 'liking' and from that many types of relationship may grow.

The reassurance aspect of disclaiming any hidden agenda may be unnecessary because it could easily be stated even if there were hidden agendas. It can be believed or not, as with ordinary conversation. There is value in it with regard to future reference: 'I thought you had no hidden agenda.'

CODE 12

12/3 *Let's try it out and see how we get on.*

This is both a reply and an invitation. It may be a reply to other codes or a direct invitation to step into a relationship.

'Let's go for a walk together.'

There is enough mutual interest to set out on the walk. Ahead there may be a sunset or a sunrise or just storm clouds.

The parties are hand in hand and not chained together. There is always time to go back or to pause.

CODE 12

12/4 *Where do we go from here? What is the next step?*

In most relationships the 'next step' simply happens. There are times, however, when things drift along. There seems to be a need for a 'next step' but neither party knows what it should be or how to state this need. The code is a convenient way for either party to state this need.

If a relationship is to move to its appropriate level (whatever that may be) there does need to be 'movement'. Code 12/4 is a suggestion that such movement could take place.

Once raised by the code the matter can be discussed in a normal way using whatever language suits.

CODE 12

12/5 *There is no hurry. Let things evolve on their own. I think things should continue as they are for the moment. There is no need for acceleration. Don't put on the pressure.*

This is not a 'back-off' signal but a plea to let things develop instead of seeking to hurry them along. It may be that there are problems to be sorted out. It may be that there is a need to get to know each other better. There is no hurry. At least that is the view of the party that uses this code.

Just as people's metabolism works at different speeds so does the metabolism of involvement.

There is also the suggestion in code 12/5 that there is some 'pressure'. The code is a clear signal that such pressure is not a good idea.

12/6 This seems to be getting a bit one-sided. I seem to be doing all the running. If you respond to my interest, please show it. Otherwise I feel I am wasting my time and just bothering you.

This is a difficult one. Some people like to be pursued and chased. They like to skip away. Some people like to be chased by several people, none of whom have a chance of getting much closer.

The code may indicate laziness or frustration. There are those who are not interested in the 'chase' and expect mutual responsiveness. There are those who are chasing hard but feeling that they are not getting anywhere.

Code 12/6 is a direct way of expressing a common-enough feeling. It may seem a little demanding.

In practice, a token of appreciation is all that is needed to keep the relationship going.

It is also common experience that 'persistence' often pays off.

CODE 12

12/7 *You are getting too intense. You are crowding me. Give me space or I shall back off. Slow down and let the relationship develop.*

In practice it is rather difficult to ask an enthusiastic person to tone down the enthusiasm. So this particular code has a high use value. It makes the point very clearly and very directly.

Eating fast does not provide better tastes than eating slowly. Some people dislike being hurried along. Everyone has a pace which suits them – similar to a 'natural' speed when driving along a road.

Should the slower person hurry up to keep up with the faster person? Or should the faster person slow down? Code 12/7 suggests the latter.

CODE 12

12/8 I am not going to ask you any questions and I do not want you to ask me any questions.

People with complicated lives do not want to be asked a lot of questions. Some people are in the habit of conducting a police-style interrogation in order to find out all there is to know. This may be well meant and may even just be a way of sustaining conversation. But private people like to be private.

The person who does not want to be asked questions may be indicating that in due course, at the proper time, all will be revealed. At the moment the answer to a question could give a false impression. It is not necessarily a matter of wanting to be secretive for ever.

A person hearing code 12/8 may choose to think the person has much to hide and is dishonest. That is a risk the code user has to take. He or she may seek to explain in ordinary language why there is a reluctance to answer questions.

The code suggests a mutual abstinence from questioning. It would hardly be fair if one party was free to ask questions and the other party was not.

The code is a perfectly legitimate request. In a court of law the past criminality of the defendant cannot be revealed at the start of a case because it would prejudice the outcome.

CODE 12

12/9 I want you to be very honest with me about your status, commitments, baggage and encumbrances.

This is almost the exact opposite of code 12/8 and is also a legitimate communication.

Many romances started on the Internet end badly when one party finds the other party is not as represented in the e-mail exchanges.

If the point is of great importance to one party then this is the code to be used. The way the other party responds may determine whether the relationship goes forward or stalls.

People have a right to ask questions. But in most circumstances they do not have a right to demand an answer. They do, however, have the right to react to the outcome.

There is always a suspicion that someone who does not want to be completely honest must have things to hide. This is not always the case. There is the matter of timing. There is also the matter of understanding complex situations. Then things can be misinterpreted.

CODE 12

12/10 *You seem to be becoming too possessive. I need space. I want to let you know how I feel.*

Very few people have any insight into how possessive they can be. It is like not knowing if you have bad breath. Only other people can tell. Should they tell you?

This code signals an 'impression'. The other party is made aware of this impression. The other party may disagree and may argue that it is not so. You can argue with the basis of a perception but you cannot argue with a perception. If things are perceived that way then they are perceived that way.

There may well be a good reason for possessiveness and even jealousy. They may even seem 'justified'. That is not the point. The code signals that this behaviour is not attractive.

CODE 12

12/11 You are becoming very demanding. I find this difficult. I feel I ought to tell you this.

Some people are indeed very demanding. They may be demanding of time, of attention, of appreciation, of gifts, etc. It may be that they need reassurance. It may be that they are greedy. Or, they may just be hyper people who need a lot of attention.

There are those who enjoy meeting endless demands. There are others who find it tiring and tiresome.

It is unlikely that someone is going to change his or her nature. So the code may only be useful at moments of great 'demand' as a sort of reminder. As with 'possessiveness', people are not usually aware they are 'demanding'. So a simple form of reminder has its value.

CODE 12

12/12 *I am in this as a romance, as an adventure, as a fling. I am not in this as a long-term commitment or investment. I thought it only fair to let you know.*

People often start with a hope of a long-term commitment and then find it is not to be. There may seem to be some point in being open and honest up front. If this is so, then code 12/12 is a simple and practical way of making this announcement.

It is true that what starts off as a romance may mature into something more solid.

The possibility of defining a relationship in advance may actually open the door to shorter relationships.

CODE 12

12/13 *I am looking for a long-term relationship or commitment. If that is not what you have in mind then I am not interested. Don't waste my time.*

Newspaper columns known as lonely-hearts columns usually have messages that make this very clear. There are people genuinely seeking a long-term relationship and marriage. This is a perfectly legitimate desire and such columns perform a very useful function.

You may hope that a relationship may indeed turn into a long-term relationship. Sometimes they do. The wastage is, however, very much less if intentions and needs are known up front.

Some people may be intimidated by the thought that they are being sized up as potential 'life partners'. Others would be delighted.

As with all other codes there is no way of ensuring honesty and avoiding abuse. Someone may come in as a 'long-term investment' but may actually have very short-term plans.

CODE 12

12/14 I like you very much and I want to be friends. Nothing more heavy than that. Friends are very valuable.

This announcement may be a disappointment to some parties but a great relief to others.

Someone who is driving north does not necessarily want to reach the North Pole. Starting a relationship does not necessarily mean an interest in a heavy, deep and long-term commitment. There is value in ease and lightness and friendship.

'Let's start a 12/14.'
'I think it best if we keep to 12/14. It is easier that way.'
'12/14 suits me perfectly.'
'I would not want to spoil a perfect 12/14 with something heavier.'

CODE 12

12/15 *I just want a small place somewhere in your life. That is all. I won't try to enlarge this place.*

There are many 'special people' in the world who we may see only occasionally but who are important to us. They may not even be good friends. But they are an important part of the whole picture.

This is a special type of relationship. Neither party seeks to change it. A niche has been established and is tended as such.

People who live rich lives have a skill in maintaining a wide variety of relationships and looking after these relationships. They have a wide repertoire of possible relationships and so can enjoy each of them. People who have only a limited view of relationships have a limited life.

CODE 12

12/16 I love you for ever – or until next Monday.

This code is slightly tongue-in-cheek. It is what Italian Romeos are supposed to say to visiting tourists. The value is that it can be said with total sincerity. After all, 'eternity' may not last longer than next Monday. Of course, the second part of the statement is said very, very quietly or under one's breath.

The beauty of this code is that it allows someone to say: 'This is what I really feel at this moment. That is totally true. But I cannot guarantee how long the feeling is going to last. Do you want to come along for the ride?'

Code 13
Relationships Continue

13/1 This relationship does not seem to be going anywhere. If we cannot move forward then I suggest we break it off. The time has come to make a decision. Things cannot go on as they are.

In many relationships one or other party eventually gets the feeling that is expressed in code 13/1. This feeling may be expressed in frequent quarrels, irritable behaviour, depression, complaints, criticism, etc. It is expected that the other party should pick up the hints, inquire as to what is the matter and learn that there is dissatisfaction.

Taking the 'next step' may mean a range of things from marriage to public acknowledgement of a relationship.

Code 13/1 expresses the feeling simply and directly. Once expressed, the matter can be discussed with ordinary language.

Note that in this code there is no hint that the relationship is boring or unsatisfactory. On the contrary, there is the implication that the relationship is so good that it ought to be taken further.
   'What is the next step?'
   'Where do we go from here?'

CODE 13

13/1

'What are we waiting for?'
'What are you waiting for?'
'Code 13/1 and I am ready to move forward.'

The intention behind code 13/1 may be seen as a suggestion; as a threat; or as a simple statement of affairs. It may be intended as any one of these – or even all three.

'Is this the way we want things to go on – for ever?'

CODE 13

13/2 This relationship has stagnated. It is getting boring. The spark seems to have gone out of it. We are drifting along. It needs some investment of energy or excitement.

Cows grazing in a field are content. No one has told them that they are bored. Would they be happier if they were told they were really bored?

There are relationships which are calm, content and not very exciting. If the people in such relationships are happy that is all that counts – no matter what other people may say. Code 13/2 does not apply to such situations.

Where one party, or both, feels that the relationship is stagnating then code 13/2 is a direct way of expressing this feeling. The other party may agree, disagree or protest.

The code can also be used in an indirect way to suggest that the other party may be becoming bored or restless. The code indicates that the relationship is stagnating, but it can be used to test the opinion of the other party.
'I feel you are becoming bored or restless.'
'It feels like 13/2 to me. What about you?'

It may be difficult to distinguish between boredom with the situation and boredom with the other person. It is up to an individual to make that distinction. The end result may be the same: code 13/2.

CODE 13

13/3 *Things are going very well. Things are getting better and better. I am very happy with the relationship. I want you to know that. I want to thank you.*

This code is upbeat, positive and appreciative.

In general we only comment on things when they are going wrong. Code 13/3 is an opportunity to praise and enjoy what is going right. It is the equivalent of saying, 'I love this relationship.' That is not exactly the same as saying, 'I love you.'

If relationships need nurturing then this is a form of nurturing.

The code may be used falsely but even false flattery has some value – it may indicate intention if not fact.

Code 13/3 is saying thank-you to the other party for the relationship.

CODE 13

13/4 *We have become complacent. We seem to take each other for granted. The relationship is drifting along. It is ticking over. Maybe that is good enough.*

The plea here is for some insight into the relationship. Let's look at it. How is it going?

This is not a suggestion that the relationship is boring or stagnant. The suggestion is that not enough attention is being given to the relationship. It is being left to look after itself.

It is like the cows in the field saying, 'Let us look at ourselves. If we are indeed happy grazing in this field, then we are happy with the way things are.'

Code 13/4 is not a complaint but more a 'maintenance' call.

13/5 Things seem to have changed. I have noticed a change in your behaviour. I need to know what is going on. I feel you are developing other interests and commitments. I need to know where I stand.

These suspicions may be groundless or they may be solidly based. The main point is that they have been 'surfaced'.

Perceptions are always real perceptions even when they do not reflect reality. So perceptions need to be attended to. The code is a way of expressing these unsettling perceptions.

Once the code has brought the matter into the open, discussion can follow. The nature of that discussion depends on the habits and needs of those involved. The code merely sets the scene and gets things going.

Overuse of code 13/5 may suggest a very insecure person who needs to be reassured all the time. It may still be better to express this through a code than through cranky behaviour.

CODE 13

13/6 *There are some important things that we need to talk about. They may be positive and negative or one or the other. But we do need to have a discussion. Can we make time for this talk?*

There may be a point in separating positive matters from negative matters with a different code for each. On the other hand, there may be more value in having a code which simply indicates: 'There are things we need to talk about.' In this way there is no anticipation of the subjects to be discussed. The guess may well be that the subjects 'needing' a talk will usually be difficulties, but that remains a guess. A few positive subjects can be thrown in from time to time!

CODE 13

13/7 *What is the problem? What has gone wrong? What are you upset about? What are you sulking about? I do not understand what is going on. Please explain.*

In this code the relationship itself is not under threat. There just seem to be difficulties which need to be faced and overcome. But there is a need to know what the problem may be.

Dealing with an unknown problem is impossible. If behaviour indicates that there may be some problem, then code 13/7 is a request that the problem be stated and clarified: 'What is the problem?'

There is some linkage here to the mood code. Some people may even want to use the mood code in such situations.

There is a sense or suspicion that something is wrong. That needs following up.

CODE 13

13/8 This is just a temporary hiccup. This is a very minor problem. Don't blow it up into a major crisis. Keep a sense of perspective. Keep a sense of proportion.

The Italians are good at having blazing rows in which the participants seem to be about to kill each other. Then twenty minutes later they are the best of friends. They seem to enjoy the hype and the drama.

There was a man who shot his wife dead because she persisted in crooking her little finger when drinking tea. Little things can become intensely irritating. They can be seen as 'signs', indications of deeper underlying problems. They can also be trivial unimportant things.

When we build up little things into big issues, we choose to do so. We do not have to make this choice. Code 13/8 is a suggestion that we do not blow things up out of proportion.

Little things may show a lack of sensitivity or a lack of consideration – but only if we choose to make those inferences.

CODE 13

13/9 *I am completely prepared to admit my fault over this matter. I am sorry. I apologize. There could have been some fault on each side but that does not matter. I am prepared to take the blame.*

This is a generous assumption of blame. Sometimes this may be fully justified. At other times the blame might have been shared. The point of the code is that it avoids allocating the blame and signals contrition.

'Whether or not I am fully to blame, I apologize fully.'

A relationship is not a court of law. The important point is not retribution but mending the relationship. The best way that would do this is the best way to take.

The henpecked husband is the one who always seems to get the blame. When this is exaggerated it becomes a caricature of itself and 'blame' loses its meaning.

CODE 13

13/10 *There you go again. Insisting on having your own way. You cannot always have your own way. You are inclined to be bossy and a bit of a bully.*

It is tiresome to keep on reminding someone that he or she is bossy. Code 13/10 provides a convenient way to do this in a more light-hearted manner.
  'A touch of 13/10, I think.'
  'It's 13/10 time again.'

Often people get into 'bossing' habits and are not even aware that their behaviour is so regarded. Code 13/10 is a reminder.

To have a whole speech about bossiness and selfishness on each occasion would be unpleasant and lead to fights. Using code 13/10 simply indicates that your behaviour could be seen in this light. Perceptions are real even if they are not reality.

CODE 13

13/11 *I feel we are making real progress and moving forward to overcome the difficulties. Thank you for that.*

This is an upbeat progress report. It is useful when there have been difficulties and problems. Even if nothing much has changed on the surface, the code signals that the basic mood may have improved.

Code 13/11 is as much encouragement as acknowledgement.

Most comments, and codes, tend to focus on the negative because that is more noticeable and that is what needs putting right. The few codes that accentuate the positive need to be used more often.

CODE 13

13/12 You know I do not like that. It annoys and irritates me. If you are not doing it on purpose then you are being careless and inconsiderate.

People have their pet hates, dislikes and irritations. These may be rational or irrational. What really annoys one person may seem trivial and harmless to another.

The code signals: 'I don't think you are trying to upset me but you have forgotten that this (action, behaviour, etc.) is very annoying to me.'

A partner who butts in on the other partner's jokes and wrecks them may see this as cooperation, but the effect can be very annoying.

As with many other codes, this one is a 'reminder' rather than a condemnation. Instead of a sharp word or a dark glance there is the simplicity of the code.

CODE 13

13/13 Don't overplay the victim. Don't overplay the martyr role.

There are people who like to claim that they are put upon and exploited. Sometimes this may indeed be true. With others it becomes a habit of behaviour: 'poor me'.

Code 13/13 is a reminder not to play that card too often.

There are people who go through life blaming everything on a miserable childhood, abuse, an accident, etc. While the event may be perfectly true, the need to blame everything on the event is often exaggerated. It is used as an excuse for everything.

The same may be true of an incident in the earlier part of a relationship. This may be brought up on every occasion as a sort of weapon.

Code 13/13 points out the exaggeration in such attitudes.

Code 14
Relationships End

14/1 *It is no one's fault but I do not think we are compatible after all. We have tried and we could try harder but in the end it is not going to work out. The fundamentals are wrong.*

If both partners feel this way then the code is merely a summary of what each knows but may not yet have expressed. If only one of the partners feels this way then the code may come as a complete surprise to the other. There is therefore a value in being able to articulate these feelings in a concise way.

The emphasis is on 'compatibility' and 'fundamentals'. The mood and the intentions may still be good and strong but if the basics are not compatible then more effort is unlikely to put things right.

There is no blame attached to either party. That is the way things are. The code is an acknowledgement of a situation.

The code is definitely not a plea to try harder and to put faults right. There is no sense of grievance – just a sense of sadness that things cannot work out.

It may be that one temperament is stifling the other. It may be that the values are totally different. It may be that the sensitivities are different. It may simply be that one partner wants children and the other one does not.

CODE 14

14/1

'Code 14/1. Is this what we both think?'
'I feel we have reached code 14/1. What do you feel?'
'Are there problems we can overcome or is it code 14/1?'

Code 14/1 is usually an acknowledgement of what both parties have been feeling for some time.

CODE 14

14/2 This relationship has been dying for some time. The spark and energy has gone out of it. Perhaps the time has come to go our separate ways. There is no special reason or explanation but flames do go out sometimes.

The difference between 14/1 and 14/2 is that in 14/1 the energy may still be there but the future looks bleak and impossible. With 14/2 the energy will have slowly evaporated. It is now simply a matter of putting the full stop at the end of the sentence.

A car tyre may have a slow leak. The result of this leak is only felt when almost all the air has gone out of the tyre. In the same way the fact that a. relationship is dying may only become noticeable right at the end. Usually, there is not even the motivation to put more air into the tyre.

Where the feeling is mutual, then the code provides a convenient acknowledgement. Where the feeling is one-sided, then the other partner really needs to know what is going on.

The danger is always that a temporary 'dip' may be misdiagnosed as a terminal decline. This is a danger however the feelings are expressed.

14/3 People change. I may have changed or you may have changed. Or we both may have changed – in opposite directions. The result is that the relationship is not working and does not make sense any longer.

People grow up at different rates. People develop in different directions. What makes sense at one time in life may not make sense at another time.

No one is to blame. It may be possible to carry on. And in some situations this may be the best course of action. In other cases, life may offer more than an inadequate relationship.

Changes in people are almost always irreversible. It becomes a matter of adjusting to the changes or walking away.

Code 14/3 acknowledges the changes and suggests it is time to walk away. Individuals may choose, instead, to stay and to adjust. The balance of feelings between the two partners will decide what happens. The code does not suggest a strategy. It is merely a summary of a situation.

CODE 14

14/4 This relationship has been dead for a long time. We both know it. We both hang on because of the fear of the unknown, because of the fear of the void out there.

Again, this code is an acknowledgement. That is the way things are (or seem to be to one party).

Perhaps habit is a sufficient basis for a relationship. Perhaps the partners have known and accepted this for a long time. Why then bring it up?

It may be brought up because one or other partner is no longer satisfied with the state of affairs and wants to end the relationship. Code 14/4 is a statement of the present situation as a preamble to some intention.

If one partner feels this way, it is rather hard for the other partner to persuade the first partner that he or she is wrong. Feelings are feelings and have their own validity.

14/5 *This is a good relationship but I think it only fair to say that I do not see any long-term future in it. We can carry on or face this possibility. It is only fair to bring this up.*

People have different needs and different agendas. Some people are happy to enjoy a good relationship for as long as it may last. Others have an eye on the future and want to settle down, have a family, etc.

Code 14/5 brings this 'time' issue to the fore. What are the long-term prospects? Is it time to think long term? What are the different time needs?

Code 14/5 may mean the start of a discussion or the beginning of the end of a relationship. The matter is out in the open.

CODE 14

14/6 *You want commitment without commitment. You want commitment to this relationship but no commitment to the future.*

This code is more of an accusation than code 14/5. One partner seems to fear commitment. The other partner is pointing this out.

It may be a decision point: 'Commit in or you are committing out!' It could be a sort of ultimatum. Ultimatums sometimes achieve their objective and sometimes they do not.

Once again, the code summarizes the complex feelings of one or other partner. There is no ambiguity.

CODE 14

14/7 I have come to the conclusion that I can't give you what you want from life. I have given it a lot of thought. I am therefore going to step aside and get out of your way so that you can get on with life. Otherwise I shall be holding you back.

There is always the hope that things will change. One partner may know that the other partner does not share the same view of the future – but hopes that that will change.

Feelings may remain the same but there can come a time when there is a need to be realistic. One or other party wants to get on with life. The present relationship is a barrier.

It is hard to let go for the sake of possible future benefits. The present benefits are present but the future benefits are mere possibilities.

It is always possible to continue on as before and let the other party make up his or her mind. There may not be a need to act on behalf of the other party.

CODE 14

14/8 *The present level of involvement is over. The relationship needs to change down to a new level. I hope we can remain friends – otherwise it has been a waste.*

There is always the hope that relationships can mature and change. Sometimes this is possible and sometimes it is not.

Code 14/8 is a clear statement that the relationship is over. The friendship aspect is a sort of compensation.

As with almost all of the other code 14 items it all depends on whether the other partner is already thinking the same way or whether it is a surprise. Feelings do change. Minds do change. People do change. Circumstances do change. Having a code to signal the type of change does not cause the change but allows it to be expressed with clarity and directness.

Accepting that a relationship is over may not be easy. Anything will be viewed as an excuse. But an excuse for what? An excuse for a change of feeling? A change of feeling should not need an excuse. Feelings are not a matter of choice or acts of will. They need to be signalled fairly and honestly.

Grumpiness and bad temper are a poor way of signalling a change of feeling.

14/9 *The plain truth is that I have met someone else. You may or may not have suspected it. It was not something I was looking for but it just happened. It is best you know now – and directly from me.*

Usually people suspect or find out that another party has become involved. Code 14/9 provides a neutral and direct way of making this plain.

Those who feel that code 14/9 is the best way out of any relationship may use this code dishonestly where there is no other person. Nevertheless there is the background intention to end the relationship and this is seen as the simplest way. Making the other party furious may be the preferred option.

On the other hand, where feelings have really evaporated it might be best to use a code that makes this clear. That kills any hope of a renewal of the relationship – even though it may seem more cruel.

CODE 14

14/10 This has happened. I am mad at you. I am disappointed. At the moment I do not know how this will work out. I may be able to forgive, if not to forget, or I may never want to see you again. I need time to think. I need space. Then we shall see.

Code 14/10 obviously refers to some particular transgression by one partner. This may end the relationship or it may be absorbed and even strengthen the relationship. At the moment the outcome is undecided.

'You have wrecked the relationship – get lost.' This could be what the code really means. Or it could mean: 'Right now the relationship seems over – but I need to think about it.'

CODE 14

14/11 The relationship has run its course. It was never meant to be a long-running event. It was great but now it is time to say goodbye.

Holiday romances might fall easily into this category – or Internet relationships. A picnic is a picnic and not a way of life.

Both parties will probably have known from the beginning that the relationship was a short-term one. It would be rather unfair for one party to know this and the other party to think otherwise. It would not be unusual for both parties to know this full well but for one party to hope that it might develop into a longer-term involvement. Code 14/11 signals the end of that hope.

CODE 14

14/12 *You are simply not the person I thought you were. You are not the person you pretended to be. Goodbye and good luck.*

People can fall in love with an image of their own creation and then blame the other party for not fitting that image.

The other party could try to fit the image but that could be a waste of effort since the pretence would need to be sustained. So it may be better to accept the separation the code signals.

The code implies a sort of accusation, yet the accusation is unfounded. If you disappoint someone's image of you then, possibly, that image was at fault.

The many ways of ending a relationship may be true in part. What matters is the need to end the relationship and to signal that end.

14/13 We could both try harder to salvage the relationship. But I feel that it is too late for that. What do you feel?

Things have not been going well. The relationship seems to be dying. Can it be saved? Do the parties want to save it? Do both parties want to save the relationship?

There are ups and downs in all relationships. The parties usually work through the downs without wanting out. A steady deterioration may be a different matter.

The code invites the other party to express his or her feelings. The matter can be discussed. If both parties feel the salvage effort is worthwhile and possible then that is the way forward. If both agree that the effort is pointless then that is the way forward. If the parties disagree the matter can be dropped for the time being.

CODE 14

14/14 *If there were an elegant and painless way to end a relationship, then I would choose that way. I do feel we ought to think about parting.*

If there were such a way out everyone would want to use it. No one likes disappointing or hurting someone else.

There do not have to be reasons for the ending of a relationship. Things evolve. Things change. The sun rises and the sun sets.

The matter can be discussed. More time and effort may be agreed. What seems like a terminal decline may be just a valley.

Occasionally, blame and reasons end relationships. More often it is just change and changed needs.

NEGOTIATION CODE 15

Negotiations range from the usual adversarial and confrontational mode to a cooperative mode in which both parties seek to design a way forward.

There is usually a lot of jockeying for position. There is a need to make suggestions and also a need to ask for things specifically. There is a need to express feelings and responses.

In negotiations standard situations repeat themselves again and again. A code provides a shorthand way of dealing with standard situations. As usual, a code also provides clarity and removes ambiguity.

A code removes the need to be emotional or to show emotions.

Just as there are formal sequences of moves in a chess game so codes can be put together to create such sequences in negotiation.

If both parties are not fully aware of the codes then code lists can be provided for both parties – or they can be put on the wall of the meeting room.

Code 15
Negotiation

15/1 Is this a genuine negotiation? Are you coming here because you need to be seen to be negotiating? Are you interested in finding a way forward or just in appearing to negotiate? Do you really just want to have your own way or are you willing to design a mutually beneficial way forward?

This may seem rather harsh and unconstructive. There are times, however, when one or other party is going through the motions of a negotiation but is not really interested in negotiating.

Of course, the response to the code will always be a protest that it is indeed a genuine negotiation. Nevertheless, the code will have indicated what one party suspects.

During the negotiation the code could also be referred to if matters are not moving forward: 'Is this a 15/1 after all?'

If there is a strong suspicion that it is not a real negotiation, then both parties can choose to play the 'tokenism' game. They can pretend to negotiate without any real intention of moving forward.

15/2 *Could you please lay out your position? What are your needs and fears? What would you like to see as the final outcome – in broad terms or in specific terms?*

This is a direct invitation to the other party to lay out their position. This might well have happened anyway or it might have been assumed that the position was well known.

At any stage in the negotiation, code 15/2 can be repeated to get the wishes of the other side.

When the wishes are expressed in very general terms there may be a need to seek clarity or more specificity. This can be done with ordinary questions within the framework of code 15/2.

It is unlikely that the other party will reveal the full position. Alternatives and fallback positions will not be revealed.

CODE 15

15/3 *You are asked to lay out what you think our position might be. What do you think are our needs and our fears? How do you see our position?*

If both sides are accurately aware of both positions then it becomes that much easier to design a way forward.

Misperceptions are the basis of misunderstanding and disagreement. It sometimes happens that one party has a very wrong impression of the other party's position.

Any expressed position can be corrected and amended as need be. This code is not unlike the attention-directing code, which directs attention to another person's views.

15/4 What can we agree upon? What do we disagree upon? What do you see as the main sticking points?

Again, this is similar to one of the attention-directing codes. The purpose of the code is to seek to narrow down the whole area of consideration to those specific points which matter most.

There may be disagreement as to the sticking points and this will lead to a useful discussion.

CODE 15

15/5 *What are the benefits that you are offering? Could you lay out the advantages or benefits for us? It is not clear where the benefits will lie.*

There are certain negotiations where there are believed to be mutual benefits. Code 15/5 is a request that these benefits be specified and clarified. Even if this is a matter of repetition, that is what is being requested.

The benefits should cover both immediate benefits and benefits into the future.

CODE 15

15/6 As it is, your offer is not attractive. You will need to increase the benefits if things are going to go further. As it stands your offer is not of interest.

If the negotiation is supposed to be for mutual benefit, then the benefits have to be accepted as mutual. If one party regards the benefits as insufficient, the matter could be at an end.

Code 15/6 could always be used as a move to extract more benefits. If this strategy is suspected, then the other party can refuse to budge.

It is always possible to ask the party using code 15/6 to suggest benefits that might be 'sufficient'.

CODE 15

15/7 These fears are real and do need to be addressed. Can we address them now?

This code emphasizes the importance of defined fears. Too often, fears that are real to one party are seen as unimportant or as a negotiating move by the other party.

Code 15/7 underlines the importance of the fears and asks that they be discussed.

Fears may be unreasonable but that does not make them unreal.

CODE 15

15/8 What is your proposal (or counter-proposal)? Please spell it out again.

This code covers both a proposal and a counter-proposal.

A proposal may be put in general terms: 'We are looking for some way of compensating those who will be made redundant.' A proposal may also be presented in detail.

There may be an overall proposal or various proposals from moment to moment.

CODE 15

15/9 What do you see as the alternatives and options at this point?

A final design may involve modifying or combining options. There does, however, need to be something to work on.

Code 15/9 asks for the basic ingredients which will form part of the agreed outcome.

A range of options can always be extended and added to. Options are possibilities and without possibilities there is no progress. Possibilities may range from the very practical to the remote.

Often, the concept behind an offered alternative can be extracted and its value delivered in a different way. This is one of the fundamental operations of creativity.

CODE 15

15/10 We have gone over the old ground again and again. Could we try to be creative and to find some really different approach? Otherwise there is a stalemate.

A plea for creativity does not by itself deliver creativity. But creative effort does produce creative results. If people set their minds to being creative they are more open to new ideas and more inclined to explore ideas which do not seem beneficial at first sight.

This plea for creativity may be followed by a formal use of lateral-thinking tools by those who know them. Or, the creative effort can stay at the more general level of the weaker brainstorming approach.

CODE 15

15/11 How do you see the future unfolding? How do you see alternative futures? What sort of things are likely to happen? What is your view of the future?

There are two sorts of future. There is the future of the world around and the changing circumstances in which the agreement may come to be played out; then there is the future as it will be affected by the terms of the agreement.

There may be best-case scenarios and worst-case scenarios. Both may need to be considered. People want to be protected from worse-case futures as much as they want to benefit from best-case futures.

15/12 *More information is needed on the following matters . . .*

This is a direct request for information on specified matters. Such information may be helpful in designing a way forward or it may be essential to taking any step forward.

The information requested should be as specific as possible. It is not much use asking for 'all the information' in some general area.

Asking for information is a common delaying tactic, so it should be explained why the information is so important.

If it seems that one party is deliberately withholding information then that information can be asked for directly.

CODE 15

15/13 At the moment I see this as rather one-sided. You want too much and are prepared to concede too little.

This might be a real perception or a pretended perception. Any party can use this code, whether it is justified or not. If it is seen as a strategic move the other party can simply ignore it: 'I am sorry you see it that way. Explain what you mean.'

In any adversarial situation, each party seeks to obtain the maximum advantage. So it is likely that from time to time matters will be one-sided.

There is also the tradition of asking for too much in the expectation that this will be reduced to what is fair.

15/14 *Are we treating this as an adversarial confrontation or are we seeking, together, to design a way forward? Perhaps we should use the Six Hats approach of parallel thinking.*

This code is more a reminder than anything else. It is very easy to slip into the 'fight' mode rather than the 'design' mode. The code is a reminder to get back into the design mode.

Those who know the Six Hats parallel-thinking method could use it to speed up discussions. Sometimes discussions can be concluded in one tenth of the time using that method.

On the one hand there is willingness to seek to work together to design a satisfactory outcome. On the other hand there are the actual thinking methods that are to be used. If people only have a repertoire of 'argument' and 'debate' then being constructive is not easy.

CODE 15

15/15 What are the contingency and fall-back positions? If things do not work out where will we be?

It is always to be hoped that things will work out according to plan. But if something goes wrong, what will the fail-safe position be?

As part of the design of the outcome it is important also to design the fall-back position.

CODE 15

15/16 Who are the people who really matter in this situation? What might their thinking be? How are they going to react?

It may be that all the key people are sitting around the negotiating table. This would be most unusual.

The union secretary has to report back to his committee and ultimately the union members. An executive might have to report back to the chief executive or the board.

An outcome that might seem satisfactory to those in the room might look very different to others who were not involved in the give and take of the negotiation but only see the final result.

Very often a leader wants to look good to his or her followers. People do not like to be seen to have backed down. Saving face might be important. All these things need to be considered and designed into the outcome.

Not all people are reasonable. Some people are show-offs. It is not a matter of wishing that people were perfect but of dealing with known imperfections.

CODE 15

15/17 *We are moving towards an outcome. What are the weaknesses in the design we have? How can those weaknesses be overcome?*

An outcome is beginning to take shape. Things are looking good. But they can be improved. The effort is to identify the weaknesses and to seek to put them right.

The effort should be a combined one by both parties. It is in the interests of both parties to have an outcome that will work.

The outcome needs to be looked at from all angles and take into consideration all possible circumstances. How does it stand up?

It may now be a matter of problem solving or further design effort. Can the benefits be enhanced? Can things be made more simple?

15/18 Is this outcome going to be acceptable? How are those outside this negotiating room going to react?

The reaction may be from shareholders in the case of a proposed merger. The reaction may be from the financial press. The reaction may be from the people identified in 15/16.

There may need to be a process of 'selling on' the outcome. Those who need to think short-term (like journalists) may not be persuaded of the long-term benefits. Those who want to use an outcome for political purposes may be less interested in the mutual benefits of an agreed outcome.

Acceptability always has to be a design consideration. It is no use choosing the material and colour you like but finding that the clothes do not fit.

The acceptability problem may affect one side more than the other. Both sides, however, need to keep it in mind if they want a satisfactory outcome. It is no use saying, 'Acceptability is your problem.'

The important design point is whether the concept of acceptability is a consideration from the beginning of the design process or is brought in at the end as a sort of cosmetic.

CODE 15

15/19 This is a stalemate. We are not getting anywhere. We do not seem likely to get anywhere. We have not made any progress (at all – or recently). We ought to acknowledge it as a stalemate and look to see how we might move forward.

The emphasis of this code is on 'acknowledgement'. The important step is acknowledgement of a stalemate.

The way forward may involve creativity. The way forward may involve abandoning a rigid position and being more flexible. The way forward may involve introducing new concepts and principles.

Going back and forth over the old ground is not likely to take things further. Blaming the other side may be justified but is not very helpful.

There needs to be a joint effort to move forward. It is not a matter of 'playing chicken' and holding out until the other side gives in.

CODE 15

15/20 Are there matters which have been left out? Have we covered all the points? Is there a need to tidy up?

This is a look around towards the end of the design process to see if all aspects have been considered. Have all values (positive and negative) had their due attention?

Matters may be left out consciously if a decision is taken that such matters are not really important. To leave out matters through neglect is a different thing.

The points need to be ticked off on some checklist. Points which may seem trivial at the time may lead to failure of the outcome later.

CODE 15

15/21 Can we review what we have discussed and what seems to have been agreed?

It may seem obvious that everyone sitting in a meeting would know exactly what has been going on. There can, however, be misinterpretations. Time spent on reviews and summaries is never time wasted.

People are rightly wary of minutes because the person writing the minutes can slip in, honestly or otherwise, matters which were not agreed upon.

Being clear in one's own mind about what has been agreed is extremely important. So having a way of asking for a review is also extremely important.

15/22 Who is going to take responsibility for what? Who is going to do what, and when? How are the agreed actions going to be taken? What is the time line?

This code directs attention to the action plan that might follow the agreement. How is the agreement going to be put into action?

The assumption is that there has been an agreement. The steps in the implementation of the agreement need to be designed, allocated and spelled out.

This aspect gives a completeness to the negotiating process. Agreement has been reached and is going to be put into action.

Occasionally, an agreement falls down at this very last step. Who is going to bell the cat? Political sensitivities may make it important to decide who is going to announce the agreement.

CODE 15

15/23 What is the next step? Where do we go from here?

There may be no agreement. So what do we do now? What is the next step? Do we give up, or try again?

Even if no other sort of agreement has been reached it might be possible to reach an agreement on the next step. Where? When? Who? What agenda?

CODE 15

15/24 That was constructive. That was good. I think we made a lot of progress. Thank you all.

This code is a sign of appreciation for all those taking part. It is a signal that progress is being made.

A final agreement may not yet have been reached but the negotiations are on track.

It is a way of saying thank-you to all the participants and the efforts they have made.

ASSESSMENT CODE 16

There are times when it is necessary to assess a performance by another person. It may be necessary to express satisfaction or dissatisfaction – or various stages in between. Just as some Inuit languages have twenty words between like and dislike, so it can be useful to have a wide range of assessment possibilities.

Code 16 provides a ready-made repertoire of assessment concepts. It is also possible to extend this range by saying, 'This is between — and —.' Or you might say, 'This is mainly — with some element of —.'

The assessment code is neutral and impersonal. It is true that a person is making a judgement but the judgement is itself defined. There is a big difference between 'making a judgement' and 'choosing a judgement'.

There need be no secret about the assessment code. Those being assessed can know the full range of assessment options that are open to them. This makes the assessment more powerful, because they know what has not been chosen.

Nothing that is subjective can be strictly fair but having the code reduces the expression of personal prejudices.

The code can equally be applied to performance of a task by an individual or team, and to general performance by an individual or a team.

Code 16
Assessment Code

16/1 This is highly competent. I cannot find fault with it. It is well done and professional.

Code 16/1 is not perfection but implies a highly competent performance. There are no obvious faults or weaknesses or things that can be picked upon.

In an examination the bulk of the papers might be highly competent. The right answers are given. The expected answers are given.

CODE 16

16/2 This is more than competent. This is excellent. There is more than expected competence. The performance is beyond competence. The performance is superb.

If competence is the acceptable base then this performance is above the baseline. Occasionally you feel not just well but 'super well'.

What has been provided is more than was expected or asked for. This is a very fine performance.

On the scale of competence this is the top end. There is no higher assessment.

CODE 16

16/3 This is both competent and highly creative. There are some powerful changes and new ideas.

The baseline of competence is there. This time what is provided above the baseline is not super-competence but creativity.

The creativity may consist of one good idea or possibility, or there may be a number of ideas.

The important point about this assessment is that the creativity is not at the expense of competence.

16/4 This is great on creativity but not so good on competence.

The competence factor may indeed be below baseline. Creativity may have been used as a substitute for competence. Or so much energy has gone into the creative aspect that the competence has been neglected.

It also happens that some people reckon that creativity is so much more important than competence that competence does not matter much.

CODE 16

16/5 *This is very patchy. Some parts are good and other parts are not good enough. The overall effect is simply not satisfactory.*

A patchy performance is a form of incompetence. The competence is not there so it is incompetence. The hopeful aspect is that it may be easier to move from a patchy performance to a competent one than from a totally incompetent performance.

Does code 16/5 imply that the performance is halfway competent? It does not. The parts that are incompetent may be the most important parts of all. If a surgeon does most of the operation well but fails to tie a bleeding artery the patient dies.

16/6 *Barely adequate. This is the bottom rung. With a lot of improvement things could become competent.*

This is 'get by' stuff. Just good enough to get by. This is basic survival but no more. This just reaches the pass mark.

Anything less would be unacceptable.

16/7 *This is a mediocre performance. It is not bad and it is certainly not good.*

The difference between 'barely adequate' and 'mediocre' lies in the motiv-ation. 'Barely adequate' implies that the person has chosen to do the minimum. 'Mediocre' implies that the person may not be capable of much more. There are some situations where the emphasis is on adequate competence. There are other situations where there is more of a spectrum from poor to excellent – and mediocre is somewhere along that spectrum.

16/8 This is a disappointing performance. You are capable of a much better performance. I expected a much better performance. This is far below your best.

This code makes a sharp distinction between performance and ability. The suggestion is that the ability is indeed there but has not been shown in the performance.

In a way this is a kind judgement but it is also a threat that a repeat of such a performance would not be tolerated. Where there is limited ability, training or knowledge, then there can be some tolerance. Where the ability is there but not used there is less tolerance.

16/9 There is a great deal of room for improvement. This performance is not good enough.

There may be an overlap between this assessment and others but this code implies that the person is 'on the right track' and with more application and training should be able to do better.

This assessment is less harsh than some others because it offers hope and emphasizes the possibility of improvement.

At times suggestions may also be given as to how the improvement may come about: experience, training, knowledge, etc.

CODE 16

16/10 *Good but full of careless errors. May be carelessness or lack of concentration.*

It may seem difficult to assess carelessness from an objective look at a performance. Usually it is the patchiness of the performance that gives the clue. A person who performs well in part should be capable of performing well everywhere – except for their carelessness.

The 'carelessness' assessment may also be a kinder way of questioning basic ability.

16/11 *Good performance but lacking in sensitivity and people skills.*

There are some tasks which involve other people. The task may be performed well but if there is a lack of people skills the result may be mixed.

There are technical tasks which do not need to involve other people, so technical brilliance is enough. At other times, and more usually, other people are involved. People skills are needed in addition to technical brilliance.

CODE 16

16/12 This is not a good performance at all. Perhaps there are reasons for this?

The performance is judged as poor. But there is a willingness to listen to excuses and reasons.

There is an acceptance of the possibility of outside factors that have prevented a better performance. So the code achieves two things. The code signals that the performance is not adequate but also signals that this may not be entirely the fault of the performer.

16/13 *This is simply a poor performance. It is not acceptable in any way. I do not want to see such a performance again.*

There is no ambiguity of suggested explanations. This is a poor performance. It is so bad that it is not acceptable.

The performance is well below the pass mark of adequacy. If the person assessing the performance does not use this judgement then he or she may not be doing their duty.

In certain circumstances a bad performance may be dangerous. In other circumstances it puts a burden on other people. Sometimes a poor performance wastes money and opportunity.

CODE 16

16/14 This is a truly shocking performance. This is plain bad. This is totally unacceptable.

This code is at the opposite end of the spectrum from code 16/2.

The person making the assessment is not interested in reasons or excuses. The performance is so bad that attention has to be on the performance itself.

CODE 16

16/15 *You may well have misunderstood what you were supposed to do. The performance is good in itself but in the wrong direction. The result is a poor performance.*

If the person performing has really misunderstood the task then the performance may have little value. Yet the ability of the person may be high. This is yet another code which offers a way out.

It is usually not too difficult to tell when a person is moving ahead – but in the wrong direction.

The misunderstanding may be the fault of the person setting the task or of the person carrying out the task. If the direction was not clear then it would be unjust to blame the doer.

Instructions that are confusing can be clarified through questioning. However, instructions that seem to point very clearly, but in the wrong direction, never get challenged.

PROJECT STATUS
CODE 17

Projects have a beginning, progress and some sort of end. Code 17 focuses on the progress of a project.

There are standard situations which can quickly be described by a code. More complex situations are treated in the usual way with verbal descriptions.

The precision of the code establishes the situation quickly and without ambiguity. Just as we recognize anything else that has a name, so we can also recognize project-status situations.

The code covers both inquiries and responses.

The code is concerned with the status of the project at the time of the inquiry.

Code 17
Project Status

17/1 What is the time status of the project? Is it on time or what?

With projects, time is often taken as a measure of success, since the different stages of success have been given different times for achievement. So asking the time status is really asking about the success of the project.

A very successful project may even be ahead of schedule. That a fast job may actually be a sloppy job is not usually considered, because quality controls are supposed to be in place.

CODE 17

17/2 *The project is behind schedule because of a number of minor problems, hiccups, delays, frictions, etc., which could have been foreseen.*

This is general sort of slippage. It may be due to a difficult task, a difficult environment, poor planning or even poor management.

The important point about the code is that there is no one major problem that has been identified and could, possibly, be solved.

There may be a need to go through matters in fine detail in order to speed up the project.

CODE 17

17/3 *There are major problems and obstacles which are holding things up. They are as follows . . .*

The single major problem or problems would then need to be spelled out. It could be environmental concern over the siting of the project. It could be an unexpected geological fault. It could be the fault of a contractor, etc.

There is a big difference between major identified problems and general slippage. Problems can be solved; slippage may need reorganization.

CODE 17

17/4 *We need help in solving the following problem or problems. We cannot solve them on our own and cannot proceed unless we solve them.*

This code is a clear request for help. It may be that the problems require political help or technical help that is not available on site.

Code 17/4 may be used directly on its own as a request for help. It is not just a reason why a project is behind schedule. It may even be used in anticipation – before a project falls behind schedule.

Asking for help may be seen as a sign of incompetence. On the other hand, knowing when help is really needed is a mark of competence.

CODE 17

17/5 *This project is resource-starved as indicated here. There are not enough resources to complete the project on schedule or to complete it at all.*

There may be a need for capital, for technical equipment, for manpower, for expertise, etc. That more resources are needed may be due to poor planning or unexpected circumstances. It may also be that another call on resources has emerged.

Code 17/5 can always be used as a handy excuse when things are not on schedule. As with several other codes there is always the danger of misuse but this is no worse than the misuse of language. It is even more obvious and blatant.

17/6 *There is some doubt about the quality of management on this project.*

Code 17/6 may be used as a question: 'Is there some doubt . . . ?' It may also be used as a statement, to mean that there is indeed some doubt.

It may be the quality of management at the most senior level or at lower levels. Obviously, senior management is not going to cast doubt on its own competence, so the code may be more generally used by others.

The code is a request to pay attention to the quality of management on the project.

CODE 17

17/7 *This project has been poorly planned. We need to replan the whole project.*

The code can be used as a question: 'Do we have a 17/7 here?' Or, it can be used as a complaint by those working on the project: 'It is a bad case of 17/7.'

Planning is fundamental to any project so a code is needed to draw attention directly to the 'planning' component.

CODE 17

17/8 The project is in crisis. We need to see how we can rescue it.

This strong diagnosis may be made by the project managers or by central headquarters. It may be in the form of a question or a judgement. 'It seems to be in crisis: is it?'

CODE 17

17/9 What is the way forward? What do you see as the next steps that need taking and that can be taken?

In short, what do you intend to do next? When two naval ships collided one commander signalled to the other: 'What do you intend to do next?' The reply came back: 'Buy a farm.'

The person asked this question may have a plan of action or may be able to put forward some options. The person may also suggest some joint thinking on the matter.

The emphasis of code 17/9 is on the next steps, not on distant destinations or generalities.

CODE 17

17/10 How do you see the future scenarios? What is the best-case scenario? What is the worst-case scenario? How will the project be affected by either scenario?

These scenarios include both the progress of the project itself and the surrounding environment. How may things work out?

Circumstances may have developed which make it highly unlikely that the project will ever succeed. It may then be best to terminate the project. On the other hand things may be moving in favour of the project, and more investment and effort will seem worthwhile.

Pictures of the future that are held by many people tend to be more credible than pictures held by individuals – but they are not necessarily more correct.

17/11 The project seems to be running low on energy. It seems to be running out of steam. Is this so? And if so, why do you think this is?

Lack of motivation, lack of energy, apathy and inertia are all different from specific problems. If there is no energy in a project it may tick over but not progress.

It may be hard to diagnose why a project has run out of energy. The simplest solution is new management. The building up of morale, team spirit and a sense of achievement all lead to more 'energy'. If a project is seen as peripheral and of low status then those working on the project may have low motivation. There is a job to be done and that is all.

The important point about code 17/11 is that there are no specific problems to be solved – although that would be easier to deal with.

The code is at the same time a suggested diagnosis, an actual diagnosis and a request for action.

CODE 17

17/12 What can I do to help? What sort of help would be most useful?

This code is a specific offer of help. It is a generic offer. It is up to the listener to indicate the sort of help that would be most useful to further the project. It is a clear signal of willingness to help.

Help is being offered. Help does not have to be asked for. It may be that the only help needed is that someone should show interest in the project.

Although code 17/12 is a clear offer of help, it could also be used as a request for help: 'It would be nice if we had a 17/12 here.'

TRAVEL CODE
CODE 18

The numeric nature of the de Bono codes makes them ideal as an international 'inter-language'. You think into the number in English and the other party thinks out of the number into Japanese, Russian, Arabic, Finnish, etc. In one fell swoop there is access to all languages.

This all depends on there being translations of the code into other languages. Once these become available the codes become truly international.

An obvious use of this internationalism is to help with travel. You express the number in writing or point to it in a book and the other person then reads out what is attached to that number.

Over time you may expect the other party to know some of the basic codes or to have their own reference book. Before that time you can carry with you the code book in the other language and simply point to the code that is needed. So if you go to China you would have your English code book and the Chinese code book. You would identify the code you wanted to use in the English book and then point to the corresponding code number in the Chinese one.

The codes may be used in combination as appropriate.

In many cases the code suggests a 'general need', which may then have to be specified in ordinary language – even in writing.

Code 18
Travel Code

18/1 *I am feeling very ill. I need to see a doctor or get to a hospital. Can you help me?*

The exact nature of the help required is not specified. To some extent this is left to the listener. It may be a matter of a doctor being called to see the patient. Or the person may be taken to a doctor or a clinic. There may even be a need to be taken to hospital.

This is left open because the organization of medical services differs greatly from one country to another.

The main point is that it is a clear request for medical help.

CODE 18

18/2 I have been robbed or am otherwise
in trouble. I need to call the police. Can you
help me?

Once again the request is general because getting police help will be easy in some countries but difficult in others.

The exact interpretation is left to the person addressed, who will know the local conditions.

CODE 18

18/3 *I am in difficulties and I need help. I need to get in touch with my embassy or consulate. I need to call them or to go there. Can you take me there or tell me how to get there?*

Three levels of help are indicated: calling the embassy; being taken there; or being told how to get there. Instead of having a code for each, it is left to the person to whom the code is addressed to decide or choose what is possible.

CODE 18

18/4 *Can you take me to . . . ? The place is indicated by one of the following additional numbers. The place can then be specified by one of the following:*

1 = my hotel
2 = this restaurant
3 = the airport
4 = the train station
5 = the bus station
6 = the hospital
7 = the embassy or consulate
8 = the main shopping area
9 = the town centre.

So 18/47 asks that the person be taken to the embassy or consulate. In the same way 18/49 asks to be taken to the town centre.

The use of the extra digit allows for greater specificity in the request.

CODE 18

18/5 *Can you tell me how I can get to the following place, as indicated by the number given.*

(The same coding applies as for 18/4.) The difference with this code is that the person is asking for information on how to get to the destination rather than asking to be taken there. So code 18/4 might be more use with a taxi driver but code 18/5 might be more use with a hotel concierge or a passer-by.

CODE 18

18/6 *I need to find accommodation. I want you to recommend a place or to take me to such a place. The type of accommodation is indicated by the number given here.*

In this case, one of the following numbers can be specified:

1 = luxury, five-star hotel
2 = four-star hotel
3 = three-star hotel
4 = two-star hotel
5 = one-star hotel
6 = small hotel of character
7 = guest house
8 = bed and breakfast
9 = cheap as possible, backpacker place.

The code may be split so the 18/6 is given first and then the specific number is given next, written down or pointed to in the code book in the other language.

CODE 18

18/7 I need to find a bank or a place where I can change money. Can you help me?

The nature of the help is not specifically indicated. The help may be a matter of pointing down the street or being given directions or being taken there.

CODE 18

18/8 *I need to make a telephone call. Where can I find a telephone?*

This is a simple request. In some countries public phones are to be found in cafés or bars. In other countries there are street phones. This can be quite confusing to a visitor.

CODE 18

18/9 I need to make an international phone call. Where can I do that?

Often there are special centres for making international calls. Making such calls from a normal phone box may be impossible or very complicated.

CODE 18

18/10 I need to connect up with my e-mail or the Internet. How can I do that?

Another communication request. There may be cyber cafés – or it may just be impossible. At least you can try.

CODE 18

18/11 *I need to send a letter or postcard to the following country. Can you sell me the right amount of stamps? Or tell me where I might get them?*

The country will need to be specified. It will also be necessary to specify the item that is to be sent.

If the place or person asked does not sell stamps then they might indicate where stamps could be bought.

This code might only have a slight advantage over holding the letter or postcard up and pointing to the stamp area.

CODE 18

18/12 Where can I find a toilet? Where is the nearest toilet?

This is such a universal need that there should be a simple universal hand sign which would immediately indicate such a need. Here is a suggestion for just such a sign.

The left hand is held palm facing downwards and the fingers together. The index and second finger of the right hand, held close together, are then placed across the knuckles of the left hand.

There is no symbolism in this sign. It is just a sign designed to be discreet but very clear.

CODE 18

18/13 Would you like to join me for a coffee, a drink, a meal or a walk? The specific request is indicated by the following additional numbers.

The numbers are:
  1 = a coffee
  2 = a drink
  3 = a walk
  4 = a meal
  5 = an evening out
  6 = show me the town.

This is a 'get to know you' code to rank alongside the other such codes in de Bono Code B.

It may or may not be easy to use. It may or may not be necessary. But it is there for convenience. Over time it may come to be used as a sort of short code for making friends.

18/14 I need to get a ticket to this destination. What do I need to do?

At a travel office, the train station or the airport, there may be a need for this code.

The code can also cover the need to change a ticket.

Obviously, there is a need to specify the destination and the preferred time of travel.

CODE 18

18/15 *I have this ticket, or this address, or this situation (pointing to something). What do I do? Where do I go? Can you tell me? Can you help me?*

This is a general-purpose request. There is some defined item, like a train ticket or an address. The person asking does not know what to do.

The request might be quite broad and could include a flat tyre. There is something that can be specified by pointing. There follows the request for information about what to do.

CODE 18

18/16 Do you speak English (or other specified language)? Does anyone here speak English? Where can I find someone who does speak English?

This is the most basic need if the rest of the communication is going to become too complex to be carried on in simple codes.

It is to be hoped that the reply will indicate someone who does speak English.

Other languages could be specified instead of English. Such other languages may be the person's native language or a second language. For example, a person's native language might be English but he or she may also speak some Italian.

Part 2

DE BONO CODE A

DE BONO CODE A

What is the logic of having de Bono Code A following de Bono code B?

The logic is very simple. In de Bono code A each number has a special meaning. In de Bono B the numbers are arbitrary and do not have any attached meaning. If de Bono code A had been placed first there would have been confusion, if someone tried to figure out the meaning of numbers which had no meaning.

Nevertheless, de Bono code A is so called because it is simpler and may well be the most used of the two codes.

THE MEANING OF THE NUMBERS

In de Bono code A each number has a special meaning. The numbers have been chosen to fit cultural sensitivities – in particular Chinese sensitivity because China will become a major user of the code in its communication with the rest of the world. For example, in Cantonese the sound of 4 is similar to the sound for 'death'. That is the reason why the numbers do not simply run: 1, 2, 3, 4, etc., as they did in the first version of the code.

Change

Imagine a tube as shown in Figure 1. Something goes into the tube and something comes out the other end. What comes out of the tube is not exactly the same as what went into the tube. There has been some change process in the tube. This simple diagram could represent any change process.

In Figure 2 we now attach a box before the change tube and a box after. The first box represents 'input' and the second box represents 'output'.

In Figure 3 we change the drawing slightly to give three boxes in a row. The middle box represents the 'change tube'.

The boxes are now numbered 1, 2 and 6.

So 1 now signifies the input. The change process is indicated by 2. The output is indicated by 6.

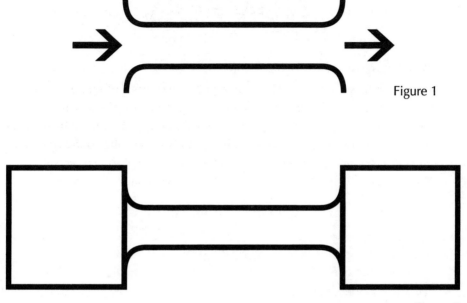

Figure 1

Figure 2

Figure 3

THE MEANING OF THE NUMBERS

System Values

There are two very general types of value: 'system positive' and 'system negative'.

System positive values are represented by a box above the 'change' box. This box is given the number 8. This is shown in Figure 4.

System negative values are shown by a box below the change box. This negative box is given the number 4. This too is shown in Figure 4.

The People Factor

The 'people factor' is indicated by the box above the output box. This is given the number 3. This represents 'people' in a very broad sense – as will be described in detail later.

The Time Factor

The 'time factor' is shown by a box below the output box. This box is given the number 9. This box represents 'time' in a very broad way. Different aspects of time are indicated by adding other numbers as will be shown later.

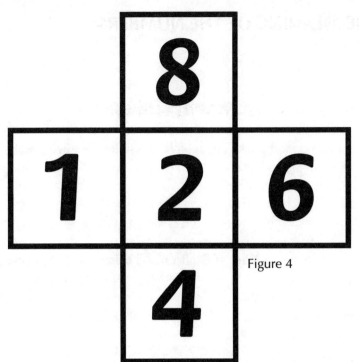

Figure 4

Figure 5

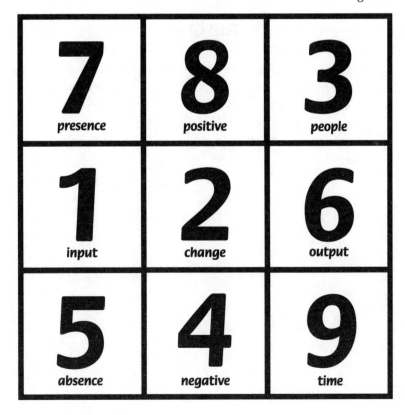

THE MEANING OF THE NUMBERS

Existence and Presence

The box above the input box represents 'presence'. This means that something is in 'existence'. It is similar to saying, 'Here is —.' Something has already come into existence.

Absence, Not Present

The box below the input box is given the number 5. This means that something is not present. Something is 'absent' or 'missing'. We know that it is missing. We note the gap or absence.

The Grid

The end result is a 3 × 3 grid with a number in each of the grid squares. This is similar to a 'noughts and crosses' grid – or 'tic tac toe' as it is known in the USA. See Figure 5.

THE USE OF DE BONO CODE A

Prefix

In order to prevent confusion between the two codes, de Bono code A should be preceded by a '00'. This is more important in written communication, and is easier than writing out 'de Bono code A'. In spoken communication the full expression can be used or the double zero prefix.

Pronunciation

Each number is pronounced directly as a single digit number. Even if there is a string of numbers each one is pronounced separately. (This is in contrast to de Bono code B where the numbers before the slash and the numbers after the slash are pronounced as full numbers, not digit by digit.) So 776 is pronounced 'seven, seven, six' in de Bono code A. There are no exceptions to this even if a coding becomes very familiar.

Overlap and Addition

De Bono code A works by overlap. The different factors or concepts provided by the basic grid are placed together to indicate that these meanings are being communicated. These 'ingredients' are all present.

Just as a painter may overlay one colour on to another to get a final shade so different concepts are laid over one another to give the final meaning.

333

THE USE OF DE BONO CODE A

The sequence in which the numbers are used does play some part – as will be seen – but the overlap is more important.

Thus 95 has the concepts of time and absence. So it means 'past tense'.

The code 96 has the elements of time and output. So this signifies the 'future tense'.

Familiarity, Reference and Use

Some of the codes will become very familiar and will enter common discourse. Everyone will come to understand them.

Other codes may need to be interpreted via a reference system as in a pocket dictionary, electronic notebook or computer (any such use is subject to licensing of the copyright).

From time to time an individual may seek to construct a meaning out of the elements for instant use. The danger is that the recipient may not get the full meaning of the intended message.

The code meanings given in this book are only a sample of the much fuller code.

7: PRESENT / THIS

The emphasis is on 'what is present'. The 7 is often used as an adjective to indicate 'this . . .'.

71   this situation

76   this outcome

79   this time; right now; at once; pronto.

78   this is good

75   this is missing; gap; need

712 this task

74   this is bad

749 this is taking too long

Make Happen

This is a special use of a double 7 as in 77. It means: 'bring into being'; 'make present'; and 'make happen'.

While 7 is passive and descriptive, 77 is very active. It is a suggestion, an order or a command.

PRESENT / THIS

776 produce a result; reach a conclusion
('make happen an outcome')

771 produce a report on the current situation

779 make time; find time

778 improve this; make better

7789 speed things up
('make, good, time')

775 remove; stop; delete
('make absent')

776 block this
('prevent an output')

772 go ahead; make the change; proceed

5: ABSENT / MISSING

Something is known, but known to be missing. It is like an empty seat at the dinner table and you know who is not there.

The 5 is often used at the beginning of a communication to ask a question.

'What is your name?' becomes: 'Your name is absent in my mind.'

53 who?

59 when?

52 how?

51 where?

577 what is going on?

56 what is the outcome?

58 what are the benefits?

54 what are the negatives?

525 what is the problem?
('why is the intended effect absent?')

When the 5 is used after another number the question aspect is lost and the 5 means that something is indeed absent or missing.

95 past tense; history

ABSENT / MISSING

25 impossible; cannot be done – or it seems so

235 automatic
('process with no people')

45 no faults; debugged

55 don't know what we don't know

1: SITUATION / INPUT / STARTING POSITION

Taken together the numbers 1 – 2 – 6 represent the change process. There is the input, then the change process and finally the result.

The present situation is represented by 1. This is where we are now. This is the input to the change process.

51   what? What is the situation?

71   the situation as specified here

714   this is a mess

771   describe this; make a report.

12   project, task or undertaking

16   connection

61   feedback

143   difficult situation because of the people

91   present tense

31   I or we

339

SITUATION/INPUT/STARTING POSITION

The 1 can be used to specify a particular project, task or thing.

1 = the bridge project
1 = the electoral campaign
1 = the proposed merger

This specification would need to be done in a side note.

2: THE CHANGE PROCESS

Anything which is not static is changing. Any sort of action, cause/effect, influence, etc., can be seen to be a sort of 'change'. If at the end something is not exactly the same as at the beginning then there is a change. If there is a change there is a change process.

Change may involve a change agent, the right environment and various supporting factors. All these are lumped together as 'the change process' and indicated by the number 6.

52   how?

22   alternatives
('changes in the change process')

772   make a change; find a way to do it

42   negative effect; damaging

525   a problem

827   solution to a problem

82   positive influence or change

12   task or project

32   operator

THE CHANGE PROCESS

233 users of a system or service

27 change (as a noun)

323 thinking
('person change person')

326 a meeting
('person change to an outcome')

28 change for the better

24 change for the worse

25 termination
('change for disappearance')

6: OUTPUT / OUTCOME / RESULT

At the end of the change process something has changed. Something is not exactly the same as at the beginning of the change process. This 'new state' is the outcome or output.

The outcome may not be the final outcome. It may be the outcome at the moment the communication is being made. The erosion of a cliff by the sea may be a continuous process going on for thousands of years. The outcome is not necessarily what will happen at the end of the process but the outcome right now.

The use of a double 6, as in 66, suggests 'possibility' or 'suppose'. Literally it means: 'an outcome produced as an outcome by our minds not by circumstances'.

56 What is the result? What is the conclusion?

65 no result; no outcome

776 produce an outcome; make a decision; reach a conclusion

86 purpose; the desired outcome

286 plan or strategy

386 person in charge; the boss

96 future tense; the future

46 danger; bad outcome

67 forecasting

26 control

343

OUTPUT / OUTCOME / RESULT

326 a meeting

('people, change, outcome')

As with the other numbers the 6 is used in a broad sense as outcome, future, result, end, purpose, etc.

8: SYSTEM POSITIVE

Essentially, the 8 means 'good' or 'beneficial'. This is a very broad value term. 'This is a good thing.'

As in many languages the 'adjective' usually comes after the noun, thus 68 (a good result).

When 'good' is almost the key factor the 8 can come first, as in 89 (good time or fast).

68 good result

38 an effective person

28 a good method or system

718 this is a good situation

282 flexibility
('good change of change')

86 purpose

89 fast

83 pleasurable

82 benefits

4: NEGATIVE /
HARMFUL /
UNFAVOURABLE / BAD

This is the 'system negative' value. The 4 is the opposite of the 8 valuation.

The basic rules for use of 4 are similar to those for the use of 8. When used purely as an adjective then the 4 follows any other number, as in 64 which means 'a bad result'.

When the negative aspect is what is focused upon more directly the 4 comes first, as in 49, which means 'slow'.

The reasons why something is unsatisfactory are not specified but could be followed up in more detail with ordinary language.

74   this is bad

714   this is a mess

64   a poor result; disappointing

24   a poor way to do things; ineffective

34   an ineffective person

54   what is wrong?

49   slow

47   error

42   bad way forward; a problem

NEGATIVE / HARMFUL

48 danger

41 poor input; high cost

The different positioning of the 4 is shown in the following usage:

34 a person who is ineffective

43 a bad person

In the first case the emphasis is on the 'person' who happens to be ineffective; in the second case the emphasis is on 'badness' which happens to be carried by a person.

3: THE PEOPLE FACTOR

The 3 directly introduces the people factor into the communication. There is no need to specify this in all situations since people are almost always involved. The 3 need only be included when there is a direct emphasis on people.

31   I or we

13   you (singular or plural)

33   they, or people in general

73   the person specified

32   the operator

326   meeting

386   person in charge; the boss

233   users of a system or service; consumers

473   human error

83   pleasurable

53   who?

63   reaction to an idea

493   time wasters

348

THE PEOPLE FACTOR

In general the 3 should be used sparingly. It is only necessary when the people factor is a key part of the communication. That there happen to be people involved is not sufficient reason for including a 'people factor'. You might as well specify daylight or night-time whenever an action is mentioned. Some things can be assumed unless they are central to the communication.

9: THE TIME FACTOR

Time is a real factor. It is not just the space within which things happen. As with the 'people factor' the 'time factor' only needs to be specified when it is a central part of the communication, as in 659 (when is the completion date?).

59 when?

69 time to completion

79 right now

89 fast

49 slow

779 make time

592 no time to do this

95 past tense

96 future tense

91 present tense

989 acceleration

94 a waste of time
('time badly used')

Everything takes time so there is no need to include the time element unless this is an important element of the communication. The code 7149 means 'this is too slow' and that is the central part of the message.

CODES A AND B: DUPLICATE AND PARALLEL

To translate single words into a poorly known language is not too difficult. But to translate complex concepts for which there is no single word is very much harder. This is where the de Bono codes come in useful.

The codes can be used in parallel with ordinary language in order to clarify the meaning and as a back-up. The same message is thereby conveyed in two different ways.

With the codes there is much less ambiguity than with ordinary language. This is particularly so with de Bono code B, which is definite. With de Bono code A there may still be some uncertainty with regard to the way the message is put together from the basic code concepts. This uncertainty will be much less than with inadequate language.

The codes can also be used to amplify what has been written or said.

The codes can be used to give an 'overview' of the thoughts on a specific topic. The details can then be filled in with ordinary language.

So there are times when the codes will be used on their own as a substitute for ordinary language. Sometimes the codes may clarify ordinary language. At other times ordinary language may elaborate what has been conveyed in the code form.

DUPLICATE AND PARALLEL

People have names because it is easier to refer to a name than to describe the role and characteristics of a person each time that person is referred to. Just as people have names so situations can come to have names. These names are the code forms.

There are the formal names of de Bono code B and the more informal (constructed) names of de Bono code A.

Part 3

INTERNATIONAL NUMBERS

INTERNATIONAL NUMBERS

Some countries (India, Gulf States, etc.) have different numbers, but world-wide the basic Arabic numerals are instantly recognizable by almost everyone. So if you were to write the numbers out the other person could immediately access the code corresponding to that number combination.

If you speak the numbers, however, the words are different in the different languages. So in conversation and over the telephone it is not possible to know what numbers are being used.

I find it truly astonishing that what I am about to suggest here has not been done before. Maybe it has been done but has not become widely used.

What I am proposing here is an 'international sound' for numbers. This means that you only need to learn ten sounds and numbers to become international in sound as well as in sight.

The sounds have been designed with the help of an acoustic engineer to be as distinct as possible.

1 = KIKKE

The 'k' sound should be sharp and the 'e' at the end should be pronounced almost as 'kikkeh'.

2 = TUTT

The 't' sound should be exaggerated. The double 't' at the end needs to be emphasized. It should be stronger than 'tut'.

3 = PEEE

The emphasis is on the exaggerated 'eee', which is prolonged, as the 'p' may be lost in poor listening conditions.

4 = DOWD

The emphasis is on the 'ow' sound. The final 'd' is fiercely pronounced as a cut-off. It is almost like 'dowdy' without the final 'y'.

5 = FEFFE

Prolongation of the 'ff' sound, like air escaping from an air mattress or a tyre. The final 'e' is pronounced in order to emphasize the final 'ff' sound.

6 = SISSI

The emphasis is on the 'ss' sound like high-pressure steam escaping. This can be prolonged. The overall sound is somewhat like 'sissy'.

7 = VOOV

The emphasis is on the 'oo' sound. At the same time the 'v' sound needs to be distinct. The final sound is somewhat like 'groove' but with a 'v' at the beginning.

8 = OTSHOY

There are two distinct sounds involved here. This could be reminiscent of the two parts of the visual 8. The second part is pronounced 'shoy' or even 'choy'. The 'y' is heavily emphasized. The first sound is a sharp 'ot' almost as if it were 'ott'.

9 = ENNE

The 'n' sound may be prolonged. The vowels are there to make this happen. So the sound goes: 'en-nn-ne'.

0 = ZOZ

The 'z' sound is pronounced as much as possible. It should not be a sharp 'z' but a prolonged one. This is like a cartoonist's idea of sleeping, 'z-z-z-z', or a bee buzzing.

INTERNATIONAL NUMBERS

Large Numbers

Each digit is pronounced as such. There is no attempt to put in hundreds, thousands, etc. So 128 is pronounced 'kikke-tutt-otshoy'; 3549 is pronounced 'peee-feffe-dowd-enne'; and 10,000,000 is pronounced 'kikke-zoz zoz-zoz-zoz zoz-zoz-zoz'.

It is not a huge task to learn ten sounds. You can also carry them on a reference card.

Once the number sounds become international then the whole code system also becomes international in speech as well as writing.

If you do not like the sounds you can also indicate the numbers with your fingers, but this would not help over the phone.

The English language is very poor at distinguishing 17 from 70 and 15 from 50. With the 'de Bono numbers' this difficulty disappears because 'kikke voov' is rather different from 'voov zoz'.

These international number sounds are not an essential part of the codes. The codes can be used without them.

(Note: these number sounds are protected by international copyright, as are all parts of this book. Licences for reproduction can be obtained.)

SUMMARY

Something of this sort is going to happen sooner or later. It is inevitable. Ordinary language is simply inadequate for the perception of complex situations. No matter how good language may be at description, this is not the same as perception.

We are trapped by the limitations of ordinary language.

In order to make much fuller use of the capacity of the human brain there is an absolute need to move to a higher-order language. This might happen very gradually over time. But there is no reason why it should not happen more sharply – as with this book.

For convenience, only part of the full codes are included in this book; they should be enough to be getting on with.

Once the coding system has been established it becomes possible to create new codes for new situations and new concepts. The door is open.

Standardization

Codes mean nothing unless they are standardized. The other party will not know what you are communicating unless there is a standard, mutually accepted code. That is why it does not make sense to have a large number of different codes running about. That would be a Tower of Babel situation.

SUMMARY

Licensing

All the material in this book is fully protected by international copyright. Individuals may use the codes directly from the book but the codes may not be reprinted, copied out, put into computers or published in any form without a formal licence – which can be obtained. Legal action will be taken against anyone who breaches the copyright.

Full details on the licensing procedure may be obtained from my web site (www.edwdebono.com) or by fax to (UK) 44 20 7602 1779 or 020 7602 1779 or (Canada) 1 416 488 544.

The copyright has to be strictly protected in order to preserve the purity of the codes and therefore their power.

In practice you may find that you only use one code or parts of a code.

In time the value of the direct coding system will become apparent: the benefits of brevity and precision will soon become obvious; the benefit of cutting across language barriers will emerge as translations are made.

Although it may not seem so at once, the ability to apprehend complex situations instantly will be a big step forward in human evolution and progress.

DE BONO CODE B

Code 1 // Pre-Code

Code 2 // Attention Directing

Code 3 // Action Code

Code 4 // Difficult Situations

Code 5 // Response Code

Code 6 // Interaction (Frantic) Code

Code 7 // Information Code

Code 8 // Youth Code

Code 9 // Meetings

Code 10 // Mood Code

DE BONO CODE B

Code 11 // Distance Code

(note: there are hand signals for this code)

Code 12 // Relationships Start

Code 13 // Relationships Continue

DE BONO CODE B

Code 16 // Assessment

Code 17 // Project Status

Code 18 // Travel Code

(note: for full details it is important to see the full code)

DE BONO CODE B

OVERVIEW OF THE CODES FROM DE BONO CODE B THAT ARE INCLUDED IN THIS BOOK

Code 1: Pre-Code

This code indicates in advance what the following message or communication is about. Like putting the question mark at the beginning of the sentence in Spanish.

Code 2: Attention Directing

Thinking tools for deliberately directing attention in order to improve perception, where ninety per cent of the errors of thinking occur.

Code 3: Action Code

A quick code which is directed at action. Communication with others or oneself.

OVERVIEW OF THE CODES

Code 4: Difficult Situations

This code classifies certain types of difficult situation so that these can be perceived and communicated. For example, a difficult environment in which to work.

Code 5: Response Code

A simplified and direct way of responding to inquiries, requests and questions. The code expresses the reply in a short manner.

Code 6: Interaction (Frantic) Code

A short code especially for dealing with 'frantic' situations between people. The code defuses the situation and removes the conflict element.

Code 7: Information Code

This code 'classifies' types of information so we know what to expect and what to look for amongst the mass of information available.

Code 8: Youth Code

Youngsters sometimes find it difficult to express awkward and embarrassing situations. The code provides a means which is neutral and comprehensive. Can be used either way between adults and youngsters.

Code 9: Meetings

A code which allows participants at a meeting to signal their thoughts and feelings visually to the speaker. So the speaker knows how they are reacting.

Code 10: Mood Code

People show their moods with facial expressions, tone of voice, behaviour and bad temper. The code provides a means of communicating a wide range of moods in a direct and quiet manner.

Code 11: Distance Code

This is a fun code which allows people to get to know each other at a distance through the hand signals which carry code 11.

Code 12: Relationships Start

The code signals different messages, intentions and moods at the start of a relationship. Instead of fumblings for words, the code provides clarity between the parties.

Code 13: Relationships Continue

This code signals situations, moods and intentions in the course of an ongoing relationship. There are things which are difficult to express with words but easy with a situation code.

Code 14: Relationships End

The relationship is coming to an end. The relationship is breaking up. These are difficult times. The way things are expressed becomes very important. The code takes over that role.

Code 15: Negotiation

In the course of a negotiation there are things each party might want to say to the other. This code formalizes some of these requests so that they become part of the negotiating process. This removes tension and aggression.

Code 16: Assessment

This code deals with the assessment of people. It is a simple and impersonal way of commenting on performance: of praising good performance and noting bad performance.

Code 17: Project Status

How is the project doing? What is holding things up? The code formalizes and simplifies communication about the status of a project.

Code 18: Travel Code

The code deals with basic requests that might need to be made across a language barrier in the course of travel: seeking accommodation; needing medical help; advice on entertainment, etc.